PHILIPPIANS AND PHILEMON

THE NEW TESTAMENT LIBRARY

Editorial Advisory Board

C. CLIFTON BLACK
M. EUGENE BORING
JOHN T. CARROLL

Charles B. Cousar

Philippians and Philemon

A Commentary

WJK WESTMINSTER JOHN KNOX PRESS
LOUISVILLE · KENTUCKY

© 2009 Charles B. Cousar

First edition
Westminster John Knox Press
Louisville, Kentucky

09 10 11 12 13 14 15 16 17 18—10 9 8 7 6 5 4 3 2 1

All rights reserved. No part of this book may be reproduced or transmitted in any form or by any means, electronic or mechanical, including photocopying, recording, or by any information storage or retrieval system, without permission in writing from the publisher. For information, address Westminster John Knox Press, 100 Witherspoon Street, Louisville, Kentucky 40202-1396. Or contact us online at www.wjkbooks.com.

Book design by Jennifer K. Cox

Library of Congress Cataloging-in-Publication Data

Cousar, Charles B.
   Philippians and Philemon : a commentary / Charles B. Cousar.—1st ed.
      p. cm.—(New Testament library)
   Includes bibliographical references and index.
   ISBN 978-0-664-22122-5 (alk. paper)
  1. Bible. N.T. Philippians—Commentaries.   2. Bible. N.T. Philemon—Commentaries.   I. Title.
   BS2705.53.C68 2009
   227'.6077—dc22

2008039356

PRINTED IN THE UNITED STATES OF AMERICA

∞ The paper used in this publication meets the minimum requirements of the American National Standard for Information Sciences—Permanence of Paper for Printed Library Materials, ANSI Z39.48-1992.

Westminster John Knox Press advocates the responsible use of our natural resources. The text paper of this book is made from at least 30% post-consumer waste.

CONTENTS

Acknowledgments	vii
Abbreviations	viii
Bibliography	x

PHILIPPIANS

Introduction to Philippians	3
Philippi: City and Church	3
The Letter: Authorship and Integrity	7
The Place and Date of Writing	9
The Character of the Letter	11
The Structure of the Letter	12
The Opponents	14
The Message of the Letter	17

Commentary

1:1–11 Introduction		**23**
1:1–2	Salutation	23
1:3–11	Prayer for the Philippians	26
1:3–8	Thanksgiving	28
1:9–11	Petition	30
1:12–26 Reassurance about the Sender		**32**
1:12–14	Paul's Imprisonment and the Spread of the Gospel	32
1:15–18a	Contrasting Preachers of the Gospel	35
1:18b–26	Paul's Anticipated Deliverance	37
1:27–2:18 Concern for the Recipients		**42**
1:27–30	To Express Unity and Courage in the Face of Opposition	42

2:1–11	To Manifest Unity and Humility after the Manner of the Christ Event	47
2:5–11	The "Christ Hymn"	50
2:12–18	Concern for the Recipients	59
2:19–30	**Travel Plans and Examples to Be Followed**	**64**
	Travelogue	64
	The Commendation of Two Models	64
3:1–4:3	**Further Exhortations and Warnings**	**67**
3:1–4a	Call to Rejoice, Warning against Mutilators, the Church as True Circumcision	67
3:4b–16	Paul's Story to Be Imitated	70
3:12–16	Identification and Acceptance of Christ's Claim	75
3:17–19	Take Note of the "Enemies of the Cross"	77
3:20–21	The Church's Heavenly Citizenship	79
4:1–3	Appeals to Steadfastness and Unity	82
4:4–23	**Closing**	**84**
4:4–9	Final Exhortations	84
4:10–20	The Matter of Giving and Receiving	87
4:21–23	Greetings and Benediction	90

PHILEMON

Introduction to Philemon   **95**

Commentary

1–3	**Salutations**	**101**
4–7	**Thanksgiving**	**101**
8–16	**Paul's Prayerful Appeal**	**102**
17–21	**Paul's Confidence in Philemon's Response**	**104**
22–25	**Paul's Travel Plans and Greetings from Friends**	**104**
	Paul and Slave Ownership	105

Index of Ancient Sources   **107**

Index of Authors and Subjects   **111**

ACKNOWLEDGMENTS

Anyone who writes a commentary on a biblical book is constantly aware of the debt he owes to others before him who have plowed the ground and have surfaced issues that otherwise are easy to ignore. My first interest in Philippians came in a class taught by my teacher and later colleague and close friend Shirley Guthrie, who conveyed a profound love for Philippians. Several classes of students have studied the book with me since Shirley's introduction, and each class has deepened my appreciation for Paul's words.

In particular, Nancy Kinzer worked closely with me on this manuscript, and Chris Henry ably constructed the indexes. I am indebted to my editors Daniel Braden and Gene Boring who pushed me to complete the project

Most of all my wife, Betty, has shown immense patience and support throughout this endeavor. During my illness she kept prodding me and saw to it that I had transportation to my office every day. To her this commentary is dedicated with much love and affection.

CHARLES B. COUSAR
EPIPHANY 2009

ABBREVIATIONS

AnBib	Analecta Biblica
ABD	*Anchor Bible Dictionary*
ANTC	Abingdon New Testament Commentaries
ASMS	American Society of Missiology Series
BDAG	Walter Bauer and Frederick W. Danker, eds., *A Greek-English Lexicon of the New Testament and Other Early Christian Literature* (3d ed.; Chicago: University of Chicago Press, 2000)
BNTC	Black's New Testament Commentaries
ET	English translation
HTR	*Harvard Theological Review*
HTS	Harvard Theological Studies
IDB	*Interpreter's Dictionary of the Bible*
Int	*Interpretation*
JBL	*Journal of Biblical Literature*
JFSR	*Journal of Feminist Studies in Religion*
JSNT	*Journal for the Study of the New Testament*
JSNTSup	Journal for the Study of the New Testament Supplements
JRelSt	*Journal of Religious Studies*
JTC	*Journal for Theology and the Church*
KEK	Kritisch-exegetischer Kommentar über das Neue Testament
KJV	King James Version
LEC	Library of Early Christianity
LXX	Septuagint
MNTC	Moffatt New Testament Commentary
NCB	New Century Bible
NCIB	New Clarendon Bible
NEB	New English Bible
NIB	*New Interpreter's Bible*
NICNT	New International Commentary on the New Testament
NIGTC	New International Greek Testament Commentary
NIV	New International Version

Abbreviations

NRSV	New Revised Standard Version
NTL	New Testament Library
NTS	*New Testament Studies*
NovT	*Novum Testamentum*
NovTSup	Novum Testamentum Supplements
OBT	Overtures to Biblical Theology
PTMS	Pittsburgh Theological Monograph Series
REB	Revised English Bible
RSV	Revised Standard Version
SBLDS	Society of Biblical Literature Dissertation Series
SBS	Sources for Biblical Study
SHAW	Sitzungen der heidelberger Akademie der Wissenschaften
SNTSMS	Society of New Testament Studies Monograph Series
TDNT	*Theological Dictionary of the New Testament*. Edited by G. Kittel and G. Friedrich. Translated by G. W. Bromiley. 10 vols. Grand Rapids, 1964–1976.
THNTC	Two Horizons New Testament Commentary
TTFL	Theological Translation Fund Library
TUGAL	Texte und Untersuchungen zur Geschichte der alt christlichen Literatur
WBC	Word Biblical Commentary
WUNT	Wissenschaftliche Untersuchungen zum Neuen Testament
ZNW	*Zeitschrift für die neutestamentliche Wissenschaft und die Kunde der älteren Kirche*

BIBLIOGRAPHY

Alexander, Loveday. "Hellenistic Letter Forms and the Structure of Philippians." *JSNT* 37 (1989): 87–101.

Bakirtzis, Charalambos, and Helmut Koester. *Philippi at the Time of Paul and after His Death*. Harrisburg, Pa.: Trinity, 1998.

Barclay, John M. G. "Paul, Philemon and the Dilemma of Christian Slave-Ownership." *NTS* 37 (1991): 161–86.

Barth, Karl, et al. *The Epistle to the Philippians*. 40th anniversary ed. Louisville, Ky.: Westminster John Knox, 2002.

Bassler, Jouette M. *Navigating Paul: An Introduction to Key Theological Concepts*. Louisville, Ky.: Westminster John Knox, 2007.

Bauckham, Richard. "The Worship of Jesus in Philippians 2:9–11." Pages 128–40 in *Where Christology Began: Essays on Philippians 2*. Edited by Ralph P. Martin and Brian J. Dodd. Louisville, Ky.: Westminster John Knox, 1998.

Bauer, Walter, and Frederick W. Danker, eds. *A Greek-English Lexicon of the New Testament and Other Early Christian Literature*. Translated by Frederick W. Danker and William Arndt. 3d ed. Chicago: University of Chicago Press, 2000.

Baur, Ferdinand Christian. *Paul the Apostle of Jesus Christ: His Life and Works, His Epistles and Teachings: A Contribution to a Critical History of Primitive Christianity*. 2d ed.; TTFL. Translated by Allan Menzies. London: Williams and Norgate, 1873.

Beare, F. W. *The Epistle to the Philippians*. BNTC. London: A&C Black, 1959.

Best, Ernest. "Bishops and Deacons: Philippians 1:1." Pages 371–76 in *Studia Evangelica. Vol. IV–V: Papers Presented to the Third International Congress on New Testament Studies held at Christ Church, Oxford, 1965*. Edited by F. L. Cross. TUGAL 102–3. Berlin: Akademie-Verlag, 1968.

———. *Paul and His Converts*. Edinburgh: T&T Clark, 1968.

Beyer, H. W. "ἐπισκέπτομαι, ἐπίσκιπος, κτλ." Pages 2:608–22 in *TDNT*. Edited by G. Kittel and G. Friedrich. Translated by Geoffrey W. Bromiley. 10 vols. Grand Rapids: Eerdmans, 1964–1976.

Bloomquist, L. Gregory. *The Function of Suffering in Philippians*. JSNTSup 78. Sheffield: JSOT Press, 1993.

Bockmuehl, Markus N. A. *A Commentary on the Epistle to the Philippians*. 4th ed. BNTC. London: A&C Black, 1997.
Bormann, Lukas. *Philippi: Stadt und Christengemeinde zur Zeit des Paulus*. Leiden: Brill, 1995.
Bosch, David Jacobus. *Transforming Mission: Paradigm Shifts in Theology of Mission*. ASMS 16. Maryknoll, N.Y.: Orbis, 1991.
Brewer, R. R. "The Meaning of *Politeuesthe* in Philippians 1:27." *JBL* 73 (1954): 76–83.
Büchsel, Friedrich. "εἰλικρινής, εἰλικρίνεια." Page 2:397 in *TDNT*.
Bultmann, Rudolf. *Theology of the New Testament*. Translated by Kendrick Grobel. 2 vols. New York: Scribner, 1951.
Caird, G. B. *Paul's Letters from Prison: Ephesians, Philippians, Colossians, Philemon: In the Revised Standard Version*. NCIB. London: Oxford University Press, 1976.
Callahan, Allen Dwight. *Embassy of Onesimus: The Letter of Paul to Philemon*. Valley Forge, Pa.: Trinity, 1997.
Calvin, John. *The Epistles to the Galatians, Ephesians, Philippians, and Colossians*. Grand Rapids: Eerdmans, 1965.
Collange, Jean-François. *The Epistle of Saint Paul to the Philippians*. Translated by A. W. Heathcote. London: Epworth, 1979.
Cousar, Charles B. *Reading Galatians, Philippians, and 1 Thessalonians: A Literary and Theological Commentary*. Macon, Ga.: Smyth & Helwys, 2001.
———. "The Theological Task of 1 Corinthians: A Conversation with Gordon D. Fee and Victor Paul Furnish." Pages 90–102 in *Pauline Theology, Volume II: 1 & 2 Corinthians*. Edited by David M. Hay. Minneapolis: Fortress, 1993.
———. *A Theology of the Cross: The Death of Jesus in the Letters of Paul*. OBT. Minneapolis: Fortress, 1990.
Craddock, Fred B. *Philippians*. Interpretation: A Bible Commentary for Teaching and Preaching. Atlanta: John Knox, 1985.
Croy, N. Clayton. "'To Die Is Gain,' Philippians 1:19–26: Does Paul Contemplate Suicide?" *JBL* 122 (2002): 517–30.
D'Angelo, Mary Rose. "Women Partners in the New Testament." *JFSR* 6 (1990): 65–86.
De Boer, Willis Peter. *The Imitation of Paul: An Exegetical Study*. Kampen: Kok, 1962.
De Vos, Craig Steven. *Church and Community Conflicts: The Relationships of the Thessalonian, Corinthian, and Philippian Churches with Their Wider Civic Communities*. SBLDS 168. Atlanta: Scholars Press, 1999.
Doughty, Darrell J. "Citizens of Heaven: Philippians 3.2–21." *NTS* 41 (1995): 102–22.
Droge, J. Arthur. "Mori Lucrum: Paul and Ancient Theories of Suicide." *NovT* 30 (1988): 63–86.

Duncan, George S. "Philippians." Pages 3:789–91 in *IDB*. 4 + supplementary vols. New York: Abingdon, 1962.

———. *St. Paul's Ephesian Ministry*. London: Hodder & Stoughton, 1929.

Dunn, James D. G. *Christology in the Making: A New Testament Inquiry into the Origins of the Doctrine of the Incarnation*. Philadelphia: Westminster, 1980.

Fee, Gordon D. *Paul's Letter to the Philippians*. NICNT. Grand Rapids: Eerdmans, 1995.

Fiore, Benjamin. *The Function of Personal Example in the Socratic and Pastoral Epistles*. AnBib 105. Rome: Biblical Institute Press, 1986.

Fitzgerald, John T. "Philippians, Epistle to." Pages 5:318–36 in *ABD*. 6 vols. New York: Doubleday, 1992.

Fowl, Stephen E. *Philippians*. THNTC. Grand Rapids: Eerdmans, 2005.

———. *The Story of Christ in the Ethics of Paul: An Analysis of the Function of the Hymnic Material in the Pauline Corpus*. JSNTSup 36. Sheffield: JSOT, 1990.

Funk, Robert W. "The Apostolic Parousia: Form and Significance." Pages 249–68 in *Christian History and Interpretation: Studies Presented to John Knox*. Edited by William Reuben Farmer et al. Cambridge: Cambridge University Press, 1967.

Furnish, Victor Paul. "The Place and Purpose of Philippians III." *NTS* 10 (1963): 80–88.

Garland, David E. "The Composition and Unity of Philippians: Some Neglected Literary Factors." *NovT* 27 (1985): 141–73.

Gaventa, Beverly R. *The Acts of the Apostles*. ANTC. Nashville: Abingdon, 2003.

———. *From Darkness to Light: Aspects of Conversion in the New Testament*. OBT. Philadelphia: Fortress, 1986.

Güttgemanns, Erhardt. *Der leidende Apostel und sein Herr: Studien zur paulinischen Christologie*. Göttingen: Vandenhoeck & Ruprecht, 1966.

Hawthorne, Gerald F. *Philippians*. WBC 43. Waco, Tex.: Word, 1983.

Hays, Richard B. *Echoes of Scripture in the Letters of Paul*. New Haven, Conn.: Yale University Press, 1989.

———. *The Faith of Jesus Christ: An Investigation of the Narrative Substructure of Galatians 3:1–4:11*. 2d ed. Grand Rapids: Eerdmans, 2002.

Holladay, Carl R. *A Critical Introduction to the New Testament*. Nashville: Abingdon, 2005.

Hooker, Morna D. *From Adam to Christ*. London: SCM Press, 1990.

———. "The Letter to the Philippians." Pages 469–549 in *The New Interpreter's Bible*. Edited by Leander Keck. *NIB* 11. Nashville: Abingdon, 1994.

Hoover, R. W. "The *Harpagmos* Enigma: A Philosophical Solution." *HTR* 64 (1971): 95–119.

Hunter, A. M. *Paul and His Predecessors*. Philadelphia: Westminster, 1961.

Hurtado, Larry W. "Jesus' Lordly Example in Phil. 2:5–11." Pages 113–20 in *From Jesus to Paul: Studies in Honour of Francis Wright Beare*. Edited by Peter Richardson and John Coolidge Hurd. Waterloo, Ontario, Canada: Wilfrid Laurier University Press, 1984.

Jeremias, Joachim. "Zu Philipper 2,7: ἑαυτὸν ἐκένωσεν," in *Abba: Studien zur neutestamentlichen Theologie und Zeitgeschichte*. Göttingen: Vandenhoeck & Ruprecht, 1966.

Jewett, Paul K. "Conflicting Movements in the Early Church as Reflected in Philippians." *NovT* 12 (1970): 362–90.

Johnson, Luke Timothy. "II Timothy and the Polemic against False Teachers: A Reexamination." *JRelSt* 6 (1978): 1–24.

Käsemann, Ernst. "A Critical Analysis of Philippians 2:5–11." *JTC* 5 (1968): 45–88.

Kennedy, Henry A. "Philippians." Pages 3:399–473 in *The Expositor's Greek Testament*. Edited by W. Robertson Nicoll. New York: Hodder & Stoughton, 1956.

Kilpatrick, G. D. "*Blepete*, Philippians 3:2." Pages 146–48 in *In Memoriam Paul Kahle*. Edited by Matthew Black and G. Fohrer. Berlin: Töpelmann, 1968.

Kittredge, Cynthia Briggs. *Community and Authority: The Rhetoric of Obedience in the Pauline Tradition*. HTS 45. Harrisburg, Pa.: Trinity, 1998.

Knox, John. *Philemon among the Letters of Paul: A New View of Its Place and Importance*. Rev. ed. New York: Abingdon, 1959.

Koester, Helmut. "The Purpose of the Polemic of a Pauline Fragment (Philippians iii)." *NTS* 8 (1962): 317–32.

Konstans, David. "Friendship, Frankness, and Flattery." Pages 7–19 in *Friendship, Flattery, and Frankness of Speech: Studies on Friendship in the New Testament World*. Edited by John T. Fitzgerald. NovTSup 82. Leiden: Brill, 1996.

Kurz, William S. "Kenotic Imitation of Paul and of Christ in Philippians 2 and Philippians 3." Pages 103–26 in *Discipleship in the New Testament*. Edited by Fernando F. Segovia. Philadelphia: Fortress, 1985.

Lampe, Peter. "Keine 'Sklavenflucht' des Onesimus." *ZNW* 76 (1985): 135–37.

Lightfoot, J. B. *Saint Paul's Epistle to the Philippians*. 8th ed. London: Macmillan, 1888.

Lincoln, Andrew T. *Paradise Now and Not Yet: Studies in the Role of the Heavenly Dimension in Paul's Thought with Special Reference to His Eschatology*. SNTSMS 43. Cambridge: Cambridge University Press, 1981.

Lohmeyer, Ernst. *Die Briefe an die Philipper, an die Kolosser und an Philemon*. 14th ed. KEK IX/1. Göttingen: Vandenhoeck & Ruprecht, 1974.

———. *Kyrios Jesus: Eine Untersuchung zur Phil. 2, 5–11*. 2d ed. SHAW 4. Heidelberg: C. Winter, 1961.

Lohse, Eduard. *Colossians and Philemon: A Commentary on the Epistles to the Colossians and to Philemon.* Hermeneia. Translated by William R. Poehlmann and Robert J. Karris. Philadelphia: Fortress, 1971.

Longenecker, Bruce W., ed. *Narrative Dynamics in Paul: A Critical Assessment.* Louisville, Ky.: Westminster John Knox, 2002.

Longenecker, Richard N. *New Wine into Fresh Wineskins: Contextualizing the Early Christian Confessions.* Peabody, Mass.: Hendrickson, 1999.

Malherbe, Abraham J. *Ancient Epistolary Theorists.* SBS 19. Atlanta: Scholars Press, 1988.

Marchal, Joseph A. "Expecting a Hymn, Encountering an Argument: Introducing the Rhetoric of Philippians and Pauline Interpretation." *Int* 61 (2007): 245–55.

Marshall, Peter. *Enmity in Corinth: Social Conventions in Paul's Relations with the Corinthians.* WUNT 2/23. Tübingen: Mohr, 1987.

Martin, Dale B. *Slavery as Salvation: The Metaphor of Slavery in Pauline Christianity.* New Haven, Conn.: Yale University Press, 1990.

Martin, Ralph P. *A Hymn of Christ: Philippians 2:5–11 in Recent Interpretation and in the Setting of Early Christian Worship.* Downers Grove, Ill.: InterVarsity, 1997.

———. *Philippians.* New Century Bible. Grand Rapids: Eerdmans, 1980.

Martyn, J. Louis, *De-apocalypticizing Paul: An Essay Focused on Paul and the Stoics by Troels Engberg-Pedersen. JSNT* 24, no. 86 (2001–2): 61–102.

Meeks, Wayne A. *The First Urban Christians: The Social World of the Apostle Paul.* New Haven, Conn.: Yale University Press, 1983.

———. "The Man from Heaven in Paul's Letter to the Philippians." Pages 329–36 in *The Future of Early Christianity: Essays in Honor of Helmut Koester.* Edited by Birger Albert Pearson et al. Minneapolis: Fortress, 1991.

Metzger, Bruce M. *A Textual Commentary on the Greek New Testament.* London: United Bible Societies, 1971.

———. *A Textual Commentary on the Greek New Testament.* 2d ed. Stuttgart: United Bible Societies, 1994.

Michael, John Hugh. *The Epistle of Paul to the Philippians.* MNTC. Garden City, N.Y.: Doubleday, 1929.

Mitchell, Margaret M. "Rhetorical Shorthand in Pauline Argumentation: The Function of the Gospel in the Corinthian Correspondence." Pages 63–68 in *Gospel in Paul: Studies on Corinthians, Galatians and Romans for Richard N. Longenecker.* Edited by L. Ann Jervis and Peter Richardson. JSNTSup 108. Sheffield: Sheffield Academic Press, 1994.

Oakes, Peter. *Philippians: From People to Letter.* SNTSMS 110. Cambridge: Cambridge University Press, 2001.

O'Brien, Peter T. *The Epistle to the Philippians: A Commentary on the Greek Text.* NIGTC. Grand Rapids: Eerdmans, 1991.

Osiek, Carolyn. *Philippians, Philemon*. ANTC. Nashville: Abingdon, 2000.
Palmer, D. W. "To Die Is Gain (Phil 1:21)." *NovT* 17 (1975): 203–18.
Peterlin, Davorin. *Paul's Letter to the Philippians in Light of the Disunity of the Church*. NovTSup 79. Leiden: Brill, 1995.
Peterman, Gerald W. *Paul's Gift from Philippi: Conventions of Gift-exchange and Christian Giving*. SNTSMS 92. Cambridge: Cambridge University Press, 1997.
Petersen, Norman R. "Philemon." Pages 291–302 in *The HarperCollins Bible Commentary*. Edited by James Luther Mays and Beverly Roberts Gaventa. Rev. ed. San Francisco: HarperSanFrancisco, 2000.
———. *Rediscovering Paul: Philemon and the Sociology of Paul's Narrative World*. Philadelphia: Fortress Press, 1985.
Pilhofer, Peter. *Philippi*. WUNT 87, 119. 2 vols. Tübingen: Mohr, 1995.
Polzin, Robert. "Literary and Historical Criticism of the Bible: A Crisis in Scholarship." Pages 99–114 in *Orientation by Disorientation: Studies in Literary Criticism and Biblical Literary Criticism, Presented in Honor of William A. Beardslee*. Edited by Richard A. Spencer. PTMS 35. Pittsburgh, Pa.: Pickwick, 1980.
Reumann, John. "Church Office in Paul, Especially in Philippians." Pages 82–91 in *Origins and Method: Towards a New Understanding of Judaism and Christianity: Essays in Honour of John C. Hurd*. Edited by Bradley H. McLean. JSNTSup 86. Sheffield: JSOT Press, 1993.
———. "Philippians, Especially Chapter 4, as a 'Letter of Friendship': Observations on a Checkered History of Scholarship." Pages 83–106 in *Friendship, Flattery, and Frankness of Speech: Studies on Friendship in the New Testament World*. Edited by John T. Fitzgerald. NovTSup 82. Leiden: Brill, 1996.
———. "Philippians 3:20–21, a Hymnic Fragment?" *NTS* 30 (1980): 594–609.
Sampley, J. Paul. *Walking between the Times: Paul's Moral Reasoning*. Minneapolis: Fortress, 1991.
Sanders, E. P. *Paul and Palestinian Judaism: A Comparison of Patterns of Religion*. Philadelphia: Fortress, 1977.
Schubert, Paul. *Form and Function of the Pauline Thanksgiving*. Berlin: Töpelmann, 1939.
Schütz, John Howard. *Paul and the Anatomy of Apostolic Authority*. With new introduction by Wayne Meeks, ed. NTL. Louisville, Ky.: Westminster John Knox, 2007.
Stanton, Graham. *Jesus and Gospel*. Cambridge: Cambridge University Press, 2004.
Steenburg, Dave. "The Case against the Synonymity of Morphe and Eikon." *JSNT* 34 (1988): 77–86.
Stendahl, Krister. *Paul among Jews and Gentiles and Other Essays*. Philadelphia: Fortress, 1976.

Stowers, Stanley K. "Friends and Enemies in the Politics of Heaven." Pages 105–22 in *Pauline Theology I: Thessalonians, Philippians, Galatians, Philemon*. Edited by Jouette M. Bassler. Pauline Theology. Minneapolis: Fortress, 1991.

———. *Letter Writing in Greco-Roman Antiquity*. LEC. Philadelphia: Westminster, 1986.

Sumney, Jerry L. *Identifying Paul's Opponents: The Question of Method in 2 Corinthians*. JSNTSup 40. Sheffield: JSOT Press, 1990.

———. *'Servants of Satan,' 'False Brothers' and Other Opponents of Paul*. JSNTSup 188. Sheffield: Sheffield Academic Press, 1999.

Tacitus. *The Annals of Tacitus*. Trans. John Jackson. Cambridge, Mass.: Harvard University Press, 1937.

Thielman, Frank. "Ephesus and the Literary Setting of Philippians." Pages 205–23 in *New Testament Greek and Exegesis: Essays in Honor of Gerald F. Hawthorne*, ed. Amy M. Donaldson and Timothy B. Sailors. Grand Rapids: Eerdmans, 2003.

Ware, James P. "'Holding Forth the Word of Life': Paul and the Mission of the Church in the Letter to the Philippians in the Context of Second Temple Judaism." UMI Dissertation Services, 1996.

White, John L. *The Apostle of God: Paul and the Promise of Abraham*. Peabody, Mass.: Hendrickson, 1999.

White, L. Michael. "Morality between Two Worlds: A Paradigm of Friendship in Philippians." Pages 201–21 in *Greeks, Romans, and Christians: Essays in Honor of Abraham J. Malherbe*, ed. David L. Balch et al. Minneapolis: Fortress, 1990.

Williams, Demetrius K. *Enemies of the Cross of Christ: The Terminology of the Cross and Conflict in Philippians*. JSNTSup 223. London: Sheffield Academic Press, 2002.

Wills, Garry. *What Paul Meant*. New York: Viking, 2006.

Winter, S. C. "Paul's Letter to Philemon." *NTS* 33 (1987): 1–15.

Wright, N. T., ed. *The Resurrection of the Son of God*. Minneapolis: Fortress, 2002.

PHILIPPIANS

PHILIPPIANS

Paul's brief but powerful letter to the Philippians reveals heartfelt warmth and acceptance between writer and implied readers. The theme of joy is pervasive throughout the letter—and this in the face of Paul's writing from prison. The apostle's prayer of thanksgiving, in this letter far more than perfunctory, includes a strong word of affection for the Philippians' participation in the gospel. At one point he addresses his readers as his "beloved and longed-for brothers and sisters," his "joy and crown" (Phil 4:1).

The reason for this outpouring of love is clear. The Philippians have repeatedly sent gifts to undergird Paul's ministry, most recently a gift borne by one of their members, Epaphroditus. Whereas in Corinth Paul had to defend himself against "false apostles" who sought to undermine his ministry and in Galatia he had to contend with agitators who preached a distorted and perverted message and who apparently attracted converts, in Philippi life and ministry have gone well. Though he calls attention to "the dogs" and "the enemies of the cross" and addresses a dispute among church members, there is no indication of either a personal attack on Paul or a wholesale departure of the Philippian Christians to a false ideology. Instead, the tone is embracing.

Indeed, of the undisputed letters of Paul, only 1 Thessalonians matches the fondness and pastoral sensitivity of Philippians. The apostle's deep feeling for his intended audience comes out in a comment to the Corinthians:

> We want you to know, brothers and sisters, about the grace of God that has been given to the churches in Macedonia. In the midst of a severe ordeal of affliction, their abundant joy and their extreme poverty have overflowed in a wealth of generosity on their part. For I testify that they gave as much as they were able, and even beyond their ability, begging us earnestly for the privilege of sharing in this ministry to the saints. And they went beyond our expectations; having given first of all to the Lord, they gave themselves by the will of God also to us. (2 Cor 8:1–5)

Introduction to Philippians

Philippi: City and Church

Philippi was a town in the northeastern area of Greece, in the territory called Macedonia. Its ancient name was Krenides, until it was rebuilt and fortified by

Philip II of Macedon, the father of Alexander the Great. Philip had foreseen the potential economic and strategic significance of the city, and when the Thracians endangered it, he took the city in 356 B.C.E. and renamed it for himself. Though small in size, Philippi was important for two reasons: its proximity to Mount Pangaion, known for its gold and silver deposits; and its location both on the Via Egnatia, which ran from Byzantium to the west coast of Greece, and near Neapolis, a port city with avenues to the sea.

An interesting textual problem surrounds the mention of Philippi in Acts 16:12. Should the text read "Philippi, which is a leading city of the district of Macedonia" (NRSV)? or should it read "Philippi, a city of the first district of Macedonia" (NRSV margin)? Since Philippi was not *the* prominent city of Macedonia (not nearly so prominent as Thessalonica), the marginal reading seems the more likely choice.[1] In either case, it is designated "a Roman colony."

Two significant battles occurred near Philippi, which sealed its character as a Roman city. In 42 B.C.E. it was the site of the famous battle in which Octavian (later Caesar Augustus) and Mark Antony defeated Cassius and Brutus. Following the battle and with the settling of many Roman soldiers there, Philippi was declared a Roman colony. In 31 B.C.E. Octavian's defeat of Antony in the battle of Actium led to a further influx of military personnel. Its status as a Roman city enabled its citizens to be free from taxation, to buy and sell property, and to be protected by Roman law. The Latin inscriptions on monuments abound.[2]

It was likely by the sea route from Troas via Neapolis that Paul, together with his companions Timothy, Silas, and possibly Luke, first arrived at Philippi (Acts

---

1. See the interesting discussion in Bruce M. Metzger, *A Textual Commentary on the Greek New Testament* (London: United Bible Societies, 1971), 444–46, where Metzger disagrees with the committee's choice.

2. There has been considerable debate in recent dissertations concerning just how Roman Philippi was in the middle of the first century C.E. Lukas Bormann, *Philippi: Stadt und Christengemeinde zur Zeit des Paulus* (Leiden: Brill, 1995), 19–24, contends that the Roman colony had a double founding, first by Mark Antony in 42 B.C.E. and second following the battle of Actium in 31 B.C.E., leaving a thousand or so military settlers in Philippi. Craig Steven De Vos, *Church and Community Conflicts: The Relationships of the Thessalonian, Corinthian, and Philippian Churches with Their Wider Civic Communities* (SBLDS 168; Atlanta: Scholars Press, 1999), 238–44, substantially agrees with Bormann, calling attention to the overwhelming number of Latin inscriptions on tombs. Peter Oakes, *Philippians: From People to Letter* (SNTSMS 110; Cambridge: Cambridge University Press, 2001), 40–76, however, constructs a detailed model of the social composition of the town. Prior to the influx of Romans, the land was in the hands of the Greeks, but when the colonization took place, the Romans displaced the Greek landowners, sending the Greeks into the city seeking economic support. Formerly modest farms were transformed into large estates. Oakes postulates that the Romans, who became the elite landowners, constituted only 3 percent of the population of the city, and only 0.6 percent would have been military veterans. The Greeks then made up the basis of the Christian community (60 percent). Peter Pilhofer, *Philippi* (WUNT 87, 119; 2 vols.; Tübingen: Mohr, 1995), 47–48, 85–92, though not engaged in the elaborate scheme of Oakes, nevertheless thinks Bormann stressed the Roman perspective too strongly and that the Christian community was basically Greek

Introduction to Philippians

16:11–12). The letter tells us nothing about the initial visit or the beginnings of the church there. All that we know comes from Acts 16:11–39.

Acts reports that on the Sabbath they gathered with a group of women "outside the gate by the river" to pray. The only person named is Lydia, "a worshiper of God," who hears what Paul has to say, and she and her household are baptized.[3] Two features about Lydia lead one to think she was financially secure. One is that she is described as "a dealer in purple cloth," a fact that in itself may not prove her prosperity. However, she owned her own home, which became the hub for the church at Philippi (16:40). A good guess is that she was unmarried or widowed, and as such, she was able to be both a merchant and the mistress of a household, and to achieve a fairly high social status in the community. Though her name begins and ends the story in Acts of Paul's stay in Philippi (16:14, 40), she is not mentioned in the letter. Two other women, Euodia and Syntyche, are identified as courageous leaders who have struggled alongside Paul "in the work of the gospel" (Phil 4:3). The three women, together with Clement and Epaphroditus, are the only people we can attach by name to this budding church.

Acts records another significant event during this stay in Philippi, and this event is also missing from the letter. On his way one day to worship, Paul encounters a slave girl with "a spirit of the python," apparently a reference to the serpent connected with the oracle at Delphi. The slave girl makes money for her owners by predicting the future and telling the fortunes for those who pay. Interestingly, she recognizes Paul and his friends for who they are. She hounds them, crying again and again, "These men are slaves of the Most High God, who proclaim to you a way of salvation" (Acts 16:17). In exasperation, Paul casts the spirit of divination out of her. The owners of the slave girl, recognizing that their source of income has dried up, drag Paul and Silas before the civic authorities and accuse them of anti-Roman behavior. The result is that the two men are severely beaten and thrown into jail.

The narrative goes on to relate how Paul and Silas begin singing and praying in jail, and suddenly about midnight an earthquake shakes the foundations of the jail, with the result that all the prisoners are freed from their shackles. The jailer awakes from his sleep in a panic, fearing that he will have to bear the burden of this jailbreak, only to hear the reassuring word of Paul that no one

---

in ethnic background. In any case, Philippi was a fairly small rural town, with a large territorium. The predominance of Latin inscriptions, the imagery on the coins, and the plan of the city certainly reflect an indelible Roman influence. See Wayne A. Meeks, *The First Urban Christians: The Social World of the Apostle Paul* (New Haven, Conn.: Yale University Press, 1983), 45–46.

3. The phrase "a worshiper of God" (or "devout") is used by Luke as a designation for a Gentile who associates himself or herself with the synagogue. Cf. Acts 13:43, 50; 17:4, 17; 18:7. See Beverly R. Gaventa, *The Acts of the Apostles* (ANTC; Nashville: Abingdon, 2003), 237.

has escaped. Amazed, he puts to Paul the critical question: "What must I do to be saved?" On learning that belief in Jesus is sufficient, he eagerly hears Paul's message. Ultimately he, together with his whole household, is baptized.

The concluding scene is intriguing. On the next morning when the magistrates declare that Paul and Silas can go free, Paul declares his Roman citizenship. The result is an apology by the magistrates for their public mistreatment of uncondemned citizens. Ironically Paul and Silas, themselves accused of anti-Roman behavior, are actually victims of anti-Roman activity on the part of the civic leaders. Paul and Silas encourage Lydia and her companions in the faith before leaving via the Via Egnatia for Thessalonica.

Without debating the historicity of all the happenings at Philippi related in Acts, several features of the story help to illumine our understanding of Philippians. First of all, the character of the Christian community there is clearly Gentile. No mention is made in the Acts account of a synagogue or of Jews. Instead of going to the synagogue, as was Paul's custom in Acts (13:5, 14–15; 17:1–2, 10; 18:4; 19:8), he locates a group of Gentile women, who have a place of prayer by the river. Since none of the names mentioned are Jewish, we are safe in judging that the church is composed primarily, if not exclusively, of Gentiles.[4]

Second, women play a prominent role in the leadership of the Christian community at Philippi. Lydia, whose entire household is baptized, hosts Paul and his colleagues, and her home becomes the center for the church. Furthermore, Euodia and Syntyche obviously have key roles to play in the life of the community. Whatever becomes of the healed slave-girl is unknown.

Third, in Acts it is clearly Paul who establishes the church in Macedonia. He is moved to do so by a vision in which a man of Macedonia pleads with Paul to "come over and help us" (16:6–10). This role as church planter is not specifically mentioned in Philippians. And yet Paul alludes frequently to his "mission in Macedonia" in his correspondence. It was repeatedly marked by opposition and suffering (Phil 1:29–30; cf. 1 Thess 2:2), which could be a reference to the occasion in which the civil magistrates flogged Paul and Silas severely and put them in the stocks (Acts 16:22–24). Yet this harsh reception hindered neither Paul's preaching of the gospel nor his development of a church in Philippi.

After Paul's initial visit to Philippi, the Philippian church members maintained ties with the apostle by sending him gifts. When he was in Thessalonica, they repeatedly supported him in his work (Phil 4:16). And again while he was in Corinth, "brothers from Macedonia" supplied his needs (2 Cor 11:9). More

---

4. Only recently has there been archaeological evidence indicating the presence of a synagogue in Philippi, and this is somewhat doubtful. It consists of an inscription on a tomb that includes the warning that if someone should put a dead body on top of the grave, he will have to pay a fine "to the synagogue." The date of the tombstone is late in the third century C.E. See Charalambos Bakirtzis and Helmut Koester, *Philippi at the Time of Paul and after His Death* (Harrisburg, Pa.: Trinity, 1998), 28–35.

recently, Epaphroditus risked his life in bearing the service that the Philippians could not in person supply (Phil 2:25–30; 4:18). It was a way for them to "share in the gospel" (1:5) and, in particular, in Paul's mission among the Gentiles. This practice of giving certainly contributed to the special affection and deep longing that Paul has for the Philippians.

The Letter: Authorship and Integrity

Only rarely in the history of New Testament scholarship has the Pauline authorship of Philippians been questioned. It bears Paul's name as writer, and echoes of the letter as Pauline can be heard in the early-second-century patristic documents (e.g., in Clement, Ignatius, Hermas, Justin Martyr, and Tertullian). It appears in the canonical lists of Marcion and the Muratorian fragment. Only Ferdinand Christian Baur in the mid-nineteenth century contended that the letter was not written by Paul because it "is characterized very definitely by monotonous repetition of what has already been said, by a want of any profound and masterly connexion of ideas, and a certain poverty of thought." One finds "no motive nor occasion for it, nor distinct indication of any purpose, or of any leading idea."[5] While today Pauline scholarship would, almost without exception, reject Baur's conclusion about who wrote the letter,[6] there remains considerable debate whether the letter has integrity or whether it may be a composite of three letters.

The case for multiple letters is primarily based on two uneven seams that expose the patchwork. The initial uneven seam is found at 3:2, where an abrupt change occurs from the theme of rejoicing to a warning about "the dogs, the evil workers, those who mutilate the flesh." Since the reader is unprepared for such a scathing attack on opponents and since 3:1 begins with the word "finally," the argument is made that 3:2–4:3 (where the theme of rejoicing is picked up again) represents a fragment of a letter that is spliced in at this point.

The second uneven seam comes in connection with the thanksgiving offered specifically for the gift brought by Epaphroditus (4:10–20). It appears so late in the letter that it seems to be an afterthought. Moreover, why did Paul wait so long to pen this thank-you? Could it represent an earlier letter written shortly after the receipt of the gift? These two uneven seams leave us with three fragments of letters: Letter A (4:10–20), Letter B (1:1–3:1; 4:4–9, 20–23), and Letter C

---

5. Ferdinand Christian Baur, *Paul the Apostle of Jesus Christ: His Life and Works, His Epistles and Teachings: A Contribution to a Critical History of Primitive Christianity* (2d ed.; TTFL; trans. Allan Menzies; London: Williams and Norgate, 1873), 59 (ET page 53).

6. Perhaps the strongest argument against Pauline authorship in recent days has been made by Darrell J. Doughty, "Citizens of Heaven: Philippians 3.2–21," *NTS* 41 (1995): 102–22, who contends that the so-called opponents mentioned in 3:2–21 fit better a post-Pauline setting, that the teachings of Paul have been universalized, and thus the author is identified as a deutero-Paulinist.

(3:2–4:3). At some point, the three fragments, all written by Paul and to the Philippian Christians, were collected together and merged into a single letter.[7]

The uneven seam between 3:1 and 3:2 admittedly presents a problem. It is possible that Paul's apology for repeating himself (3:1b) is an allusion to the oral messages brought by Epaphroditus and Timothy,[8] though it is more likely that the apology serves as a conventional introduction to the exhortations that follow. One of the characteristics of hortatory material is the assurance to readers that they are not ignorant, that they are merely being reminded of something they already know and are not being confronted with new demands.[9] Furthermore, I contend in the commentary that the reference to "the dogs, the evil workers, and the mutilators of the flesh" is not a polemic against a threatening group in Philippi, but the holding up of a negative example to the readers. This approach makes the uneven seam seem not so uneven.

Third, the location of the thanksgiving at the end of the letter (4:10–20) forms an *inclusio* with the thanksgiving at the beginning (1:3–11) and thus need not be separated off as a distinct letter. Gerald Peterman highlights the numerous parallels between the two sections, proving rather conclusively that 4:10–20 is not the only place in the letter where Paul expresses his thanks to the Philippians.[10]

Fourth, the prayer of thanksgiving (1:3–11) introduces topics that run throughout the three fragments, suggesting a unified composition and a cohesiveness that defy the notion of multiple letters pieced together. Themes that appear in all the fragments—joy, Paul's contentment in the face of his trials, the apostle's confidence that the Philippians will endure their trials, the importance of unity, the mutual sharing of sufferings—make the fragments appear not so fragmentary.[11] Of particular importance are the definite parallels between chapters 2 and 3. David E. Garland highlights the striking connection of vocabulary as well as themes in these chapters.[12]

Finally, one has to ask whether the uneven seams at 3:1–2 and 4:10–20 can best be explained as a part of a single letter or by some theory of multiple com-

---

7. Another scheme of interpreting the material also concludes with three letters but divides them differently. Letter A is the brief thanksgiving (4:10–20); Letter B explains Paul's circumstances in prison and urges solidarity in the church (1:1–3:1; 4:4–7; 21–23); Letter C is polemical, written to counter the opponents (3:2–4:3; 4:8–9). See Carl R. Holladay, *A Critical Introduction to the New Testament* (Nashville: Abingdon, 2005), 520.

8. See Victor Paul Furnish, "The Place and Purpose of Philippians III," *NTS* 10 (1963): 86–88.

9. Stanley K. Stowers, "Friends and Enemies in the Politics of Heaven," in *Pauline Theology I: Thessalonians, Philippians, Galatians, Philemon* (ed. Jouette M. Bassler; Pauline Theology; Minneapolis: Fortress, 1991), 115–16.

10. Gerald W. Peterman, *Paul's Gift from Philippi: Conventions of Gift-exchange and Christian Giving* (SNTSMS 92; Cambridge: Cambridge University Press, 1997), 90–98.

11. See the commentary at 1:3–11 for a full listing of these topics.

12. David E. Garland, "The Composition and Unity of Philippians: Some Neglected Literary Factors," *NovT* 27 (1985): 157–59.

Introduction to Philippians

positions. Why would an editor have created the rough transitions that one admittedly finds in the letter? How is one to explain the sloppy job of editing by the one who drew the three fragments together? As Hooker puts it, "It is easier to attribute the sudden changes to Paul than to an editor!"[13]

Thus I shall work with the letter as a single document and offer commentary along the way to help in understanding the uneven seams.

The Place and Date of Writing

Repeatedly while writing Philippians, Paul speaks of being imprisoned (1:7, 13, 14, 17; literally "in chains"). In fact, one of the reasons for writing the letter apparently is to inform his Christian friends in Philippi of his current situation, namely that his imprisonment is turning out for the advancement of the gospel.

But where is Paul imprisoned when Epaphroditus brings him the gift from the Philippians, and from where he does he write this letter? He does not indicate directly in the letter, since the Philippians would know where he is incarcerated, nor does he even give many hints so that modern readers can easily figure out where he is imprisoned. Three options have been proposed.

Traditionally, Rome is thought to be the location from which all the so-called prison letters[14] were written. The book of Acts closes with Paul's being under house arrest in Rome (28:16–31), and the references to "the whole praetorian guard" (Phil 1:13) and to Caesar's household ("the emperor's household," 4:22) fit the context nicely (though these groups could also be found in other Roman-controlled towns). Whether or not the communication and travel back and forth between Philippi and Rome, presumed in the letter, could have occurred is debatable. This would have involved four trips: word that Paul is a prisoner has to reach Philippi; Epaphroditus comes to Rome; word gets back to Philippi that Epaphroditus is ill; word comes to Paul and Epaphroditus that the Philippians are worried about him. While there may have been overlapping movements in the communication trips between Philippi and Rome, the issue of distance (eight hundred miles, a journey taking up to two months[15]) cannot be ignored.

More problematic, however, is the scuttling of Paul's missionary plans that would have to occur. When writing Romans, Paul's intentions are to go to Jerusalem, then to Rome, and "with no further work" for him in the Eastern regions to turn his attention westward to Spain (Rom 15:22–29). If, however, when he writes Philippians, he intends to visit them soon (Phil 2:24), then he has markedly changed his plans and no doubt has given up the prospects of a

---

13. Morna D. Hooker, "The Letter to the Philippians," in *The New Interpreter's Bible* (ed. Leander Keck; *NIB* 11; Nashville: Abingdon, 1994), 472.
14. Ephesians, Philippians, Colossians, and Philemon.
15. Hooker, "Letter," 474.

mission in Spain. Philippians 1:25–26 hardly indicates that he has "no further work" in Macedonia. While Paul on occasion did change his travel plans, this would have been a significant shift in missional strategy for him and something he would likely have addressed in the letter.[16]

A second proposal for Paul's imprisonment is Caesarea. Though there is no mention in his letters of his being imprisoned there, Acts does record an imprisonment in Caesarea just prior to his going to Rome (Acts 23:23–26:32). Paul could have planned to visit Philippi on his way to Rome and thus not have necessarily abandoned his intentions to go to Spain. While the distance between Caesarea and Philippi is the longest of any of the three cities being considered, Acts has Paul stay in Caesarea long enough for the travels to have taken place. The major problem with Caesarea is that there is no threat of imminent death during Paul's imprisonment there and no expectation of a coming verdict (as reflected in Phil 1:20–26).[17]

A third proposal for Paul's imprisonment is Ephesus. While no specific mention of an imprisonment in Ephesus can be found in Acts or the letters, Paul indicates that he has been imprisoned many times (2 Cor 6:5; 11:23) and particularly refers to an imprisonment in Asia (2 Cor 1:8–10). The apocryphal *Acts of Paul* mentions a weeklong incarceration in Ephesus. Moreover, the comment "We despaired of life itself. Indeed, we felt that we had received the sentence of death" (2 Cor 1:8–9) reflects the mood of Philippians (especially Phil 1:19–24). There seems to be little doubt that the size and importance of Ephesus would have necessitated the presence of a Roman provincial headquarters there, as well as a detachment of the praetorian guard. When Paul sends greetings from "the emperor's household" (4:22), he could easily be referring to an imperial civil service, consisting of freedmen and slaves with administrative responsibility. Such local jurisdictions were found throughout the empire. Of the three options, Ephesus is the closest to Philippi, and one could easily account for the coming and going reflected in the letter. If the letter were written from Ephesus, then the travel plans set out in Romans 15, including a mission to Spain, would not need to be altered significantly. Finally, there is no hint in the letter that Paul has been back to Philippi since his initial visit mentioned in Acts 16, which leaves Ephesus as the least problematic of the three options.

---

16. Among those commentators holding to the Roman imprisonment are J. B. Lightfoot, *Saint Paul's Epistle to the Philippians* (8th ed.; London: Macmillan, 1888), 1–46; Gordon D. Fee, *Paul's Letter to the Philippians* (NICNT; Grand Rapids: Eerdmans, 1995), 34–37; Markus N. A. Bockmuehl, *A Commentary on the Epistle to the Philippians* (4th ed.; BNTC; London: A&C Black, 1997), 30–32.

17. Primary advocates of the Caesarean origin of the letter are Ernst Lohmeyer, *Die Briefe an die Philipper, an die Kolosser und an Philemon* (14th ed.; KEK IX/1; Göttingen: Vandenhoeck & Ruprecht, 1974), 3–4, and Gerald F. Hawthorne, *Philippians* (WBC 43; Waco, Tex.: Word, 1983), xxxvi–xliv.

Any definite choice between the three cities, however, leaves the reader with unanswered questions. Rome and Ephesus seem more likely choices than Caesarea, and commentators tend to be equally divided. If Rome were the place of imprisonment, then Philippians would likely be the last of Paul's letters and dated around 60–64 C.E. If Ephesus were the place from which the letter is sent, then it would be written much earlier (about 52–55 C.E.), and Romans would be the last letter written by the apostle. Ephesus seems the better choice and the one I use in the commentary.[18]

The Character of the Letter

While the most obvious reason for writing a letter in the ancient world was to communicate information, letters served a number of purposes. An ancient theorist writing under the pseudonym of Demetrius lists twenty-one types of letters and provides samples for each.[19] For example, one could write to issue orders, to mediate a dispute, to threaten or praise someone, to urge a particular style of behavior, or to nurture friendship with the reader(s). A writer could choose one or another type of writing, in part based on his or her relationship to the reader(s) (whether writing to a socially inferior or superior person, to a family member, to a social equal), on the current state of the relationship, and on the particular reasons for writing.[20]

What about Philippians? On the one hand, it seems obvious that the letter is Paul's thank-you to the Philippians for their gift to him (4:10–20) and that for some reason Paul thinks it necessary to commend Epaphroditus, who has been the bearer of the gift and who is now returning to Philippi (2:25–30). On the other hand, Paul reports on his situation in prison (1:12–26) and encourages both unity and steadfastness on the part of the Philippians, who face the same struggles he has faced (1:27–2:18).

---

18. An increasing number of recent commentators opt for the Roman imprisonment as the place for writing the letter. See Peter T. O'Brien, *The Epistle to the Philippians: A Commentary on the Greek Text* (NIGTC; Grand Rapids: Eerdmans, 1991), 18–26; Fee, *Philippians*, 34–37; Bockmuehl, *Philippians*, 25–31; Hooker, "Philippians," 473–75. For a Caesarean imprisonment, see Lohmeyer, *Briefe*, 3–4, 15–16; Hawthorne, *Philippians*, xli–xliv. Commentators who contend for an Ephesian imprisonment include John Hugh Michael, *The Epistle of Paul to the Philippians* (MNTC; Garden City, N.Y.: Doubleday, 1929), xii–xxi; Jean-François Collange, *The Epistle of Saint Paul to the Philippians* (trans. A. W. Heathcote; London: Epworth, 1979), 15–19; George S. Duncan, "Philippians," *IDB*, 3:789–91; Carolyn Osiek, *Philippians, Philemon* (ANTC; Nashville: Abingdon, 2000), 29–30; Frank Thielman, "Ephesus and the Literary Setting of Philippians," in *New Testament Greek and Exegesis: Essays in Honor of Gerald F. Hawthorne* (ed. Amy M. Donaldson and Timothy B. Sailors; Grand Rapids: Eerdmans, 2003), 205–23.

19. See Abraham J. Malherbe, *Ancient Epistolary Theorists* (SBS 19; Atlanta: Scholars Press, 1988), 30–41.

20. Stanley K. Stowers, *Letter Writing in Greco-Roman Antiquity* (LEC; Philadelphia: Westminster, 1986), 51–57.

More recently, it has been argued that while Paul may have had more than a single reason for writing, the basis for understanding the cohesiveness of the letter comes from Paul's choice of "a hortatory letter of friendship" as the model for communication.[21] Certainly the letter is packed with the language and conventions of friendship. Examples are the absence-presence motif (1:19–26; 2:12), expressions of affection and the desire to be with the readers (1:7–8; 4:1), the reciprocity between writer and readers (1:7, 30; 2:17–18; 4:14), the pattern of giving and receiving (4:10–20), the importance of mutual participation (*koinōnia*, 1:5; 2:1; 3:10; 4:15), the push for agreement and equality (1:27–2:4; 4:2), the need for a single mind (2:2, 5; 4:2), and the sharing of common enemies (1:27–30; 3:2, 17–19).

Noting these conventions of friendship, however, does not necessarily prove that Paul has followed a literary and rhetorical category called "a letter of friendship." The words *philia* and *philos* do not appear at all in the letter, and as Reumann notes, "There is something of a jump from the mood created by certain words and phrases to a proposed letter form. Philippians ill fits the examples of such a letter type in the theorists' handbooks, and one wonders if such letters ever were written and were not simply for schoolboy exercises and a classification scheme seldom found in 'pure' form."[22] Thus it seems a bit confusing to identify Philippians as "a hortatory letter of friendship." If the label does no more than simply call attention to friendship conventions and motifs in the letter, then all is well and good. If, however, one assumes that Paul follows a specified letter form in composing Philippians, then the term is misleading.

The Structure of the Letter

In many respects Philippians follows the pattern of other Pauline letters. Its salutation is familiar and is followed by a prayer of thanksgiving and petition for Paul's readers. The body of the letter begins with a disclosure expression ("I want you to know, brothers and sisters"), a characteristic Pauline way of introducing the body of letters (see Rom 1:13; 2 Cor 1:8; Gal 1:11; and 1 Thess

---

21. Several scholars have identified Philippians as "a letter of friendship," each building on the research of predecessors. See Peter Marshall, *Enmity in Corinth: Social Conventions in Paul's Relations with the Corinthians* (WUNT 2/23; Tübingen: Mohr, 1987); L. Michael White, "Morality between Two Worlds: A Paradigm of Friendship in Philippians," in *Greeks, Romans, and Christians: Essays in Honor of Abraham J. Malherbe* (ed. David L. Balch et al.; Minneapolis: Fortress, 1990), 201–21; Stowers, "Friends and Enemies"; John T. Fitzgerald, "Philippians, Epistle to," *ABD*, 5:318–26; Fee, *Philippians*, 2–14.

22. John Reumann, "Philippians, Especially Chapter 4, as a 'Letter of Friendship': Observations on a Checkered History of Scholarship," in *Friendship, Flattery, and Frankness of Speech: Studies on Friendship in the New Testament World* (ed. John T. Fitzgerald; NovTSup 82; Leiden: Brill, 1996), 105.

Introduction to Philippians

2:1). Furthermore, the conclusion contains traditional features, such as the sending of greetings and a benediction.

Loveday Alexander calls attention to the structure of familial letters in the Greco-Roman context and notes the significant parallels to Philippians. Following the opening address and a prayer for the recipients, the writer reassures the readers about his or her own situation ("I am in good health and prosperity, though I do not know where I shall be going from here") and then requests reassurance about the readers' welfare ("Please send word about how it goes with you. Take care of yourself."). Philippians follows this pattern, in that after the opening address and the prayers of thanksgiving and intercession, the apostle reports on his circumstances in prison (1:12–26) and then turns to the situation of the readers (1:27–2:18).[23]

In addition to following the familial structure whereby the writer reports on his own situation before inquiring about the plight of his readers, Paul uses an inordinately high number of exhortations to encourage the Philippians in their task to remain faithful and steadfast (1:27; 2:2–4, 12–15: 4:4–6, 8–9). He foresees dark clouds on the horizon for his original readers and urges them to maintain a unified front in the face of their adversaries (1:27–30). His way of inquiry into their situation is given voice in an eagerness to hear that they are living a life worthy of the gospel (1:27), that they are standing firm in one spirit and are in no way intimidated by their opponents (1:27), and that they are of one mind, doing nothing from selfish motives (2:2–4).

One form of exhortation that appears often in Philippians is the use of models, both positive and negative, to advocate a particular style of life. Ancient rhetoric employed models frequently. For example, Pseudo-Labanius offers the advice, "Always be an emulator of virtuous men. For it is better to be well spoken of when imitating good men than to be reproached by all when following evil men" (*Epistolary Styles*, 52). Further examples abound in the hortatory letters of Seneca, Pliny, and the Socratics.[24] Of course, Christ is the primary model to be followed, particularly in light of his death and exaltation, something we examine in detail in connection with 2:6–11. The reader of Philippians finds the imitation motif also in connection with Timothy (2:19–23), Epaphroditus (2:25–30), and

---

23. Loveday Alexander, "Hellenistic Letter Forms and the Structure of Philippians," *JSNT* 37 (1989): 87–101. The parallels are more obvious in the Greek than in the English text. The Greek of 1:12 reads *ta kat' eme* ("the things concerning me"), whereas the Greek of 1:27 reads *ta peri hymōn* ("the things concerning you").

24. For further examples, see Luke Timothy Johnson, "II Timothy and the Polemic against False Teachers: A Reexamination," *JRelSt* 6 (1978): 1–24; Benjamin Fiore, *The Function of Personal Example in the Socratic and Pastoral Epistles* (AnBib 105; Rome: Biblical Institute Press, 1986), 79–163; William S. Kurz, "Kenotic Imitation of Paul and of Christ in Philippians 2 and Philippians 3," in *Discipleship in the New Testament* (ed. Fernando F. Segovia; Philadelphia: Fortress, 1985), 103–26.

Paul himself (3:17), whereas negative models to be avoided are "the dogs, the evil workers, those who mutilate the flesh" (3:2), and those who "live as enemies of the cross" (3:18). The rhetorical impact is accentuated when positive and negative models are juxtaposed to one another (so 2:21–22; 3:2–4; 3:18–20).

The following analysis of the structure of the letter seeks to take account of the numerous exhortations as well as the parallels with familial letters.

I. Introduction (1:1–11)
   A. Salutation (1:1–2)
   B. Prayer for the Philippians (1:3–11)
      1. Thanksgiving (1:3–8)
      2. Petition (1:9–11)
II. Reassurance about the Sender (1:12–26)
   A. Paul's Imprisonment and the Spread of the Gospel (1:12–14)
   B. Contrasting Preachers of the Gospel (1:15–18a)
   C. Paul's Anticipated Deliverance (1:18b–26)
III. Concern for the Recipients (1:27–2:18)
   A. To Express Unity and Courage in the Face of the Opposition (1:27–30)
   B. To Manifest Unity and Humility after the Manner of the Christ Event (2:1–11)
   C. To Work for Wholeness and Faithfulness as a Community (2:12–18)
IV. Travel Plans and Examples to Be Followed (2:19–30)
   A. The Coming of Timothy to Philippi (2:19–23)
   B. The Anticipated Coming of Paul to Philippi (2:24)
   C. The Return of Epaphroditus to Philippi (2:25–30)
V. Further Exhortations and Warnings (3:1–4:3)
   A. Call to Rejoice, Warning against Mutilators, the Church as True Circumcision (3:1–4a)
   B. Paul's Story to Be Imitated (3:4b–16)
   C. Take Note of the "Enemies of the Cross" (3:17–19)
   D. The Church's Heavenly Citizenship (3:20–21)
   E. Appeals to Steadfastness and Unity (4:1–3)
VI. Closing (4:4–23)
   A. Final Exhortations (4:4–9)
   B. The Matter of Giving and Receiving (4:10–20)
   C. Greetings and Benediction (4:21–23)

The Opponents

A great deal of scholarly attention has been devoted to determining exactly who are Paul's and the Philippians' opponents. At four points in the letter there is

Introduction to Philippians

specific evidence that a group or groups stand in opposition to the apostle, the readers, or the gospel itself. It is critical, if possible, to identify these groups and to clarify the nature of their opposition.

1. In 1:15–18 Paul mentions persons who preach the gospel but do so "out of envy and strife.... They preach Christ out of selfish ambition, not genuinely but intending to add to my suffering during my imprisonment." This group is contrasted with another group who preach because of God's will, "out of love, knowing that I have been put here for the defense of the gospel." Paul is remarkably charitable toward the former group, saying that for whatever reason the gospel is being preached and in that he rejoices.

Robert Jewett has proposed that these preachers who compete with Paul were itinerants, who believe that valid apostles should exhibit extraordinary phenomena such as having ecstatic visions and working miracles.[25] Since Paul's humiliating imprisonment left him far short of qualifying as an apostle, they preached in competition with him. But would Paul be so generous in his comments about them, acknowledging that they at least preach the gospel? He certainly was not so accepting with regard to a similar group in Corinth ("Even Satan disguises himself as an angel of light!"[26]). About all one can say for sure about the group in 1:15–18 is that it operates not primarily in Philippi but wherever Paul is imprisoned and that we do not know what provokes the rivalry and ill will toward the apostle.

2. In 1:27–30, following an exhortation that the readers "live as citizens worthy of the gospel of Christ," Paul urges them to stand firm in one spirit and in no way to be intimidated by their opponents. Two features of the text lead one to think that the Roman civil authorities in Philippi represent the opposition here. First, the Greek word "live as citizens" (*politeuesthe*) comes from the political arena, and its connotation would not be lost on readers who lived in a Roman colony. They are exhorted by the apostle to "live as citizens worthy of the gospel of Christ" (1:27). As Bockmuehl writes, "Against the colonial preoccupation with the coveted citizenship of Rome, Paul interposes a counter-citizenship whose capital and seat of power are not earthly but heavenly, whose guarantor is not Nero but Christ."[27] This sets the readers in opposition to Rome.

The second exegetical point is the recognition that Paul identifies the readers' situation with his own struggle: "which you saw I had and now hear that I still have" (1:30). Whether or not Acts 16:19–24, which gives us an account of his persecution at the hands of the Roman magistrates provoked by the local merchants, is precisely what Paul has in mind in 1:30, his (and their) "struggle" likely had to do with non-Christians and with civil (and not religious) authorities.

---

25. Paul K. Jewett, "Conflicting Movements in the Early Church as Reflected in Philippians," *NovT* 12 (1970): 362–90.
26. 2 Cor 11:14; cf. 2 Cor 11:12–13; 12:12; 13:1–2.
27. Bockmuehl, *Philippians*, 98.

3. A third group often listed as opponents are "the dogs, the evil workers, those who mutilate the flesh " (3:2). Two exegetical details are important in clarifying the nature of these "opponents." Some time ago G. D. Kilpatrick made the case that the Greek verb *blepō* means "beware" only when followed by an objective clause with a subjunctive mood verb ("beware lest") or by the preposition *apo*, and that otherwise it carries a softer meaning, such as "take note of," "consider," or "pay attention to."[28] Thus Paul is advising the readers to "look at" or "consider" these people, but in doing so, he is not being polemical, as if they represent an immediate threat to the readers. His tone appears more parenetic than harsh.[29]

But why then these epithets that seem to be name-calling?[30] "Dogs" was a pejorative term used often to denigrate people (1 Sam 17:43). In the main, a dog was "the most despicable, insolent, and miserable of creatures."[31] The word "workers" may refer to missionary activity (see Matt 9:37–38; 10:10), though in this instance, they are called "evil workers." The third expression, "the mutilation (*katatome*) of the flesh," is a play on the word "circumcision" (*peritomē*) and underscores the sarcastic use of the first two terms. Thus, these three invectives are turned on their heads to insult the superiority of those who are proud of their "works," who exclude Gentiles, and who care only about keeping themselves pure. The three terms gain strength in that they appear alliteratively in the Greek language, each beginning with the letter "k" ("*kynas*," "*kakous*," "*katatomē*"). Taken together, this threefold description amounts to a denial of "the proudest claim" of the Jewish people.[32] Who these Jews were and where they lived (not likely in Philippi) remain mysteries. They are simply being held up as a negative model for the readers, especially in light of the contrasting comment, "For we are the circumcision."[33]

4. The mention of a fourth group opposed to Paul and the Philippians comes later in chapter 3, when following his autobiographical witness to the gospel Paul speaks of those who live as "enemies of the cross of Christ" (3:18). They are further described with these negative comments, "Their end is destruction; their god is the belly; their glory is in their shame; their minds are set on earthly

---

28. G. D. Kilpatrick, "*Blepete*, Philippians 3:2," in *In Memoriam Paul Kahle* (ed. Matthew Black and G. Fohrer; Berlin: Töpelmann, 1968), 146–48.
29. Stowers, "Friends and Enemies, 116.
30. Koester, "Purpose," 318.
31. Hurtado, "Jesus' Lordly Example."
32. Hooker, "Philippians," 11:524.
33. Jerry Sumney concludes "that they are opponents who are not a part of the Philippian congregation." They "seem to be traveling Christian preachers who require Gentiles to be circumcised. It also appears that, in spite of the abusive epithets, they are making little or no headway in Philippi, because Paul can present them as negative examples. We cannot specify what they claim is gained through circumcision" (Jerry L. Sumney, *Identifying Paul's Opponents: The Question of Method in 2 Corinthians* [JSNTSup 40; Sheffield: JSOT Press, 1990], chap. 5, p. 4).

matters" (3:19). The general nature of these descriptive accounts opens the door to considerable speculation as to who these folks are. Are they the same people as those mentioned in 3:2? In using "cross" terminology, is Paul's purpose "to challenge notions of what he perceives as power, privilege, charisma, and individual accomplishment that are counter-productive to his view of the eschatological community"?[34] Does the reference to "the belly" imply libertinism, or its opposite, the strict observance of food laws? What connection is there between this group and the exhortation to "imitate" the apostle (3:17)?

However one answers these questions, it is clear that the "opponents" in sections 1, 3, and 4 above are not treated as a threat to the Philippians, and thus should probably not be labeled "opponents." In fact, the case can be made that the real "opponents" to Paul, the Philippians, and the gospel were the civil authorities, mentioned in 1:27-30. They are a group that is making life hard for the Philippians and for Paul. References to the "dogs, the evil workers, the mutilation of the flesh" and the "enemies of the cross" in chapter 3 serve as negative examples, and the two contrasting preachers of the gospel in 1:15-18 are a part of Paul's report on the progress of the gospel during his imprisonment.

The Message of the Letter

It is impossible to abstract a theology from the text of any Pauline letter, and yet because of the nature of a commentary and the way it is normally used (i.e., commentaries are rarely read straight through, from beginning to end), it is necessary to provide clues as to what sort of message the letter conveys to the readers.

Basically, four primary purposes motivate the apostle to pen the letter: (1) He reports on his situation in captivity to ease the anxieties that the Philippians might have about him and to assure them of the "advancement of the gospel" through his "chains" (1:12-26). (2) He wishes to express gratitude to the Philippians for their recent gift to him, brought by Epaphroditus (4:10-20). (3) He feels it necessary to commend Epaphroditus to them for his labors and to urge the Philippians to receive him back with honor (2:25-30). (4) Anticipating the persecution that the readers will soon undergo, he takes the opportunity to encourage them to remain united and to stand firm in the face of aggressive opposition (1:27-30) and an internal dispute (4:2-3).

But how does Paul go about fulfilling these purposes, particularly in light of the numerous exhortations given? The answer is that Philippians is a community-building letter in which the apostle seeks to mold the thinking of his readers in a distinctively Christian way. The verb *phroneō* (to think, in terms of practical reasoning) occurs an inordinately high number of times in the letter, which

---

34. Demetrius K. Williams, *Enemies of the Cross of Christ: The Terminology of the Cross and Conflict in Philippians* (JSNTSup 223; London: Sheffield Academic Press, 2002), 8.

would indicate that Paul is seeking to fashion the mind of the community so that it will conform its life to Christ's death. He writes to encourage a distinctive way of thinking among his readers.

The case can be made that Paul has a similar objective in writing 1 Corinthians (see 1 Cor 1:18–2:16, where Paul seeks to reorient the Corinthians' way of thinking).[35] The context in Corinth, however, differs greatly from that in Philippi. The Corinthian community is badly divided (1:1–17), and other issues plague the church as well. In Philippi, however, Paul writes to a group of believers who have shared in the work of the gospel and have evidenced only a minor dispute (Phil 4:2–3).

It may be that what is looming large for the implied reader is the opposition posed by the imperial powers of Rome. Paul's use of "gospel" in chapter 1 is seemingly set over against the rival "gospels" declared by the imperial authority. In the hymn of 2:6–11 Jesus is given the name that is above all other names, the name of power, "Lord Jesus Christ." While Paul does not directly address the political authorities, much in the letter makes sense against the background of the imperial cult.

From the beginning of the letter to the Philippians, a story[36] is told that reaches back to "the first day" the readers heard and responded to the gospel (1:5), that includes the present time of suffering and opposition (1:28–30), and that looks forward to "the day of Jesus Christ" (1:6, 10; 2:16). As the readers seek to live blameless and innocent lives, holding forth the word of life (2:16), their focus is toward the future. Their citizenship is in heaven (3:20). Rather than being preoccupied with earthly things, the community's mind is to be fashioned by Christ, whose arrival it eagerly awaits (3:20–21; 4:5).

The primary figure in this eschatological framework is Jesus Christ. Especially in the so-called Christ hymn of 2:6–11 we read Christ's story, telling how he was in the form of God, but did not count equality with God as something to be exploited. Instead he emptied himself and took the form of a slave. He humbled himself and was obedient unto death on a cross. Therefore, God exalted him to a high place and gave him a superior name that would precipitate the worship of him as Lord by all God's creatures.

This story of Christ in turn plays both a direct and an indirect role in the letter. As the drama of God's saving event, it is intended directly to shape the thinking and life of the community (2:5). The text does not ask that an extraordinary virtue, such as humility, be abstracted from the story and made a virtue to be emulated. Rather the whole story, including the eschatological worship of Jesus

---

35. See Charles B. Cousar, "The Theological Task of 1 Corinthians: A Conversation with Gordon D. Fee and Victor Paul Furnish," in *Pauline Theology, Volume II: 1 & 2 Corinthians* (ed. David M. Hay; Minneapolis: Fortress, 1993), 90–102.

36. For a discussion of epistle-as-narrative, see *Narrative Dynamics in Paul: A Critical Assessment,* ed. Bruce W. Longenecker (Louisville, Ky.: Westminster John Knox, 2002).

Introduction to Philippians

as Lord, takes on a mind-shaping role. To be sure, the Christ hymn serves a parenetic function to exhort the readers to look not to their own interests but to the interests of others, but the hymn does not stop with verse 8. It goes on to depict God's exaltation of Christ and the giving to him of the name of power—Lord. One cannot realistically expect to be humble simply because one assumes Christ as a model of humility. Only as Paul's readers live in a world where the hostile powers are being subjected to the kenotic[37] Christ can they expect to live in humility with one another. Verses 9–11 state that such a time is on the horizon.

Indirectly, the Christ hymn also provides the language for the other models called on in the letter—Paul (sharing Christ's sufferings by conformity to his death; 3:10), Epaphroditus (coming close to death, risking his life for the work of Christ; 2:30), and Timothy (seeking not his own interests but the interests of others; 2:20–21). In each case, the story of Christ functions as "a generative image" for the individual model as for the thinking and living of the entire Philippian community.[38]

In two other passages in the letter, Paul's christocentric perspective comes to the fore. First, in 1:21–22 he faces the prospect of release from prison or possibly death. If he is released, then living means Christ. On the other hand, if he is killed, then dying is gain; that will mean more of Christ. Then in 4:11–14, as he thanks the Philippians for their gifts to him, he takes a Stoic-like attitude toward the ups and downs of human life: "In any and all circumstances I have learned the secret of being well-fed and of being hungry, of having plenty and of being in need" (v. 12). Though he doesn't specifically mention how he is enabled to face the prosperity and hardships dealt him, it is clear that "the one who strengthens" him is Christ (v. 13).[39] Interestingly, this significant Christ shapes the *koinōnia* within the community, a participation in the gospel marked by unity (1:28; 2:1–2; 4:2), humility (2:3–4), and steadfastness in the face of opposition (1:28; 4:1).

Finally, the message of Philippians is inadequately stated if it does not call attention to the theme of joy. Eleven times the verb "rejoice" (*chairō*) and five times the noun "joy" (*chara*) appear in this short letter. It is remarkable that the theme should be repeated so often when Paul, the writer, is imprisoned, and the readers are facing serious opposition. "Joy" describes the overwhelming feeling Paul has for his readers at their participation in the gospel (1:4; 4:1, 10), an

---

37. That is, the kenotic Christ is the one who emptied himself and became obedient unto death, even death on a cross.

38. Wayne A. Meeks, "The Man from Heaven in Paul's Letter to the Philippians," in *The Future of Early Christianity: Essays in Honor of Helmut Koester* (ed. Birger Albert Pearson et al.; Minneapolis: Fortress, 1991), 335–36.

39. It is interesting that some manuscripts have undergone scribal emendations with the name "Christ" added, obviously to clarify the one who strengthens Paul. (See Codex Alexandrinus and Codex Bezae.)

experience they can have in receiving Epaphroditus back into their community with honor (2:28–29), and even when they demonstrate steadfastness in the face of opposition (2:17–18). The fact that the apostle can attach the adverb "always" to the exhortation to "rejoice" means that he is urging his readers to embrace a constant stance of joy, no matter what the circumstances.

COMMENTARY

1:1–11 Introduction

1:1–2 Salutation

The letter begins in the usual manner of ancient letter writing by indicating the name(s) of the sender(s) and the recipient(s), followed by a greeting or salutation (1:1–2). Paul then expresses his thanksgiving for the Philippian Christians (1:3–8) and offers a petition to God for their life together, that it may be marked by an overflow of love and discernment (1:9–11). Though typical of the literary conventions of the day, the opening is rich with theological meaning and in specific ways reflects themes to be developed later in the letter.

> 1:1 Paul and Timothy, servants of Christ Jesus, to all the saints in Christ Jesus who live in Philippi, together with the overseers and deacons.
> 2 Grace to you and peace from God our Father and the Lord Jesus Christ.

[1:1–2] Several features of this opening warrant special comment. First, though the letter is undoubtedly written by Paul (see the shift to the first-person singular in 1:3), Timothy is listed as a co-sender. This should come as no surprise since, of the seven undisputed letters of Paul, five are coauthored (1 and 2 Cor, Phil, 1 Thess, Phlm), and in all but one, the coauthor is Timothy (the exception being 1 Cor). Of the six disputed letters of Paul, two list Timothy as a coauthor (Col, 2 Thess), and of course two letters are addressed to Timothy (1 and 2 Tim).

With each particular letter, the question to be asked is: why was Timothy listed as a co-sender when he obviously did not compose the letter? We note the important role Timothy played as Paul's missionary companion and the special task he is assigned in connection with the Philippian church (2:19–24). Though Acts does not explicitly name Timothy in connection with the founding of the church there (Acts 16:11–40), he is listed in connection with Paul's missionary activity throughout Macedonia (Acts 16:1–5; 17:14–15). With some justification, Collange postulates, "It could be precisely because Timothy appeared as one of the apostle's assistants, no more, that right from the start he invests him with his own authority in view of the mission as his plenipotentiary to that city to which he is going to entrust to him (Phil 2:19–24)."[1] His function in being

---

1. Collange, *Philippians*, 144–45.

an apostolic representative is thus strengthened when he is listed as co-sender of the letter.

Second, instead of using his most frequent self-identification, "apostle(s) of Jesus Christ" (Rom 1:1; 1 Cor 1:1; 2 Cor 1:1; Gal 1:1), Paul refers to himself and to Timothy as "servants or slaves [*douloi*] of Jesus Christ." There were no major conflicts between himself and the Philippians that would have warranted his need to claim the apostolic label, as was the case with the Corinthian letters, and thus Paul seems to choose a title for himself (and his companion) that describes the way he sees himself. What specifically does he connote by identifying himself (and Timothy) as *douloi Christou Iesou*? Is the title chosen, as Bloomquist contends, to set before the Philippians the nature of Paul's ministry, that is, his sufferings for the church?[2] The expression then would become a means of Paul's establishing credibility with his audience. Or does the title come from its common meaning as "indentured servants," in which case the stress would fall on the humility Paul senses in his relationship to Jesus Christ? He then "implied by his choice of the word *douloi* that both he and Timothy were totally at the disposal of their Master."[3]

What these two explanations fail to recognize is that the term "servant" or "slave" of Christ Jesus is widely used throughout the New Testament as an authoritative title for Christian leaders. Derived from the Old Testament (Num 12:7; Jer 25:4; Amos 3:7; Neh 10:29; 2 Kgs 14:25; Ps 89:20 [LXX: 88:21], where Moses, David, Jonah, and the prophets are called *douloi*), the title appears in the salutations of three of the general letters (Jas 1:1; 2 Pet 1:1; Jude 1) and in Titus (1:1). Furthermore, in the disputed letters of Paul, Epaphras is called a "slave of Christ" (Col 4:12) and Timothy a "slave of the Lord" (2 Tim 2:24). In none of these contexts is the notion of self-effacement or humility a primary concern. Dale Martin comments, "The very fact that so many early Christian authors use 'slave of Christ/God' for those very figures they wish to hold up as authoritative proves that the term was not heard as self-effacing. It was a title of authority and power by association."[4] While not self-effacing, the title may denote something of Paul's vision of mission in relation to the "overseers and deacons." Since Paul's authority is unquestioned in Philippi, he could be depicting a style of leadership that has to do with service and not with promotion of the self or with even a benign despotism.

The letter is addressed "to the saints who live in Philippi, together with the overseers and deacons" (1:1). "Saints" or "holy ones" (*hagioi*) appears in the letter openings of three other undisputed letters of Paul (Rom 1:7; 1 Cor 1:2; 2

---

2. L. Gregory Bloomquist, *The Function of Suffering in Philippians* (JSNTSup 78; Sheffield: JSOT Press, 1993), 36.

3. O'Brien, *Philippians*, 45.

4. Dale B. Martin, *Slavery as Salvation: The Metaphor of Slavery in Pauline Christianity* (New Haven, Conn.: Yale University Press, 1990), 51.

Cor 1:1) and is an equivalent to *ekklēsia* (church). The holiness that sets the community apart is found in Christ (1 Cor 1:30), and is not an inherent virtue of the people.

What is most unusual about the addressees is the mention of "overseers and deacons." It represents the only use of *episkopos* in the undisputed letters of Paul. In secular writings it appears frequently as a nontechnical term for one who has oversight of goods, children, or tutors, a usage that even goes back to the time of Homer. The work of a ship's captain or merchant was to oversee and protect the goods entrusted to his care (Hom. *Od.* 8, 163). Antiochus Epiphanes "appointed commissioners [overseers, *episkopous*] over all the people" to see that his orders were obeyed (1 Macc 1:51). The fundamental idea of protective care, oversight, or inspection thus lies at the root of the word.[5] In the New Testament the only place where the word clearly designates an office in the church is 1 Tim 3:1–2.

On the other hand, the term "deacon" (*diakonos*) seems to connote an office at an earlier stage than "overseer" (*episkopos*). Phoebe is referred to as a "deacon" in Rom 16:1; Paul and Apollos are called "deacons" in 1 Cor 3:5; and even Paul's opponents are called "deacons" in 2 Cor 11:23. It may be wise to think of a "deacon" in the early church as one who serves in a special way as determined by the needs of the particular community, such as leadership in the worship or pastoral care or service activity of the congregation. The role of a deacon would likely vary from location to location.

The appearance of these two terms at the outset of the letter is a bit of an anomaly. Why should they be singled out in this particular context? Peterlin argues that the "overseers and deacons" are somehow involved in a rift within the church. Euodia and Syntyche (4:2–3), he contends, are deacons and prosperous patronesses, and the conflict that emerges between them has to do with providing financial support for Paul's ministry.[6] These women are singled out

---

5. H. W. Beyer, "ἐπισκέπτομαι, ἐπίσκοπος, κτλ.," *TDNT*, 2:608–22; Lightfoot, *Philippians*, 95–99. Reumann has made the intriguing proposal that the title *episkopos* is an adaptation from the Greco-Roman environment, as a supervisory officer of the state with financial responsibilities. See John Reumann, "Church Office in Paul, Especially in Philippians," in *Origins and Method: Towards a New Understanding of Judaism and Christianity: Essays in Honour of John C. Hurd* (ed. Bradley H. McLean; JSNTSup 86; Sheffield: JSOT Press, 1993), 82–91.

6. Davorin Peterlin, *Paul's Letter to the Philippians in Light of the Disunity of the Church* (NovTSup 79; Leiden: Brill, 1995), 101–32. Ernest Best takes both "bishops" and "deacons" to be officials in the church and poses the possibility that Paul was responding to a letter from "all the saints, together with the bishops and deacons," implying a distinction between "all the saints" on the one hand and "the bishops and deacons" on the other hand. In his reply, Paul forgoes his usual title "apostle," which might have reinforced with his readers a hierarchical pattern, and instead he declares that he serves God in a lowly fashion, as a "slave of Jesus Christ." According to Best, Paul employs a "little mild irony" in addressing his readers. See Ernest Best, "Bishops and Deacons: Philippians 1:1," in *Studia Evangelica, Vol. IV–V: Papers Presented to the Third International Congress on*

from the beginning because the letter has primarily to do with them and their inability to agree on matters of importance within the congregation.

We deal with the problems between Euodia and Syntyche in the commentary on 4:2–3; however, suffice it to say now that no evidence in the letter indicates that these two women carry the title of "overseer" or "deacon." Furthermore, it is not at all clear that the disunity among the Philippians that underlies Peterlin's proposal actually exists. The warmth with which Paul addresses the Philippians, particularly at the beginning of the letter (1:3–11), would seem strange if he intended to deal with a major division within the congregation.

While the early church has not reached any sort of developed polity at the time of the writing of Philippians, what we are seeing is the beginnings of a structured leadership that varies from situation to situation, depending on the needs of the church and upon the gifts and talents of the members. As Meeks indicates, there was likely a three-tiered pattern in the church at large: apostles; co-workers (such as Timothy, Aquila, and Prisca); and the local leaders.[7] At the local level the lists of leaders and their functions are broader and less specific (1 Cor 12:8–10, 28–30; Rom 12:6–8; Eph 4:11).

In the salutation (1:2), Paul may have used a wordplay on the usual epistolary *charein* ("greetings") by using *charis* ("grace"). If so, it becomes a regular practice since it appears frequently in the openings of his letters. "Grace" is God's "merciful 'Nevertheless'" that is spoken to the fallen and lost creation,[8] and which provides the context in which believers now stand (Rom 5:1–2). "Peace" likely reflects the Hebrew root *shalom*, implying wholeness and well-being. The source of both grace and peace is "God our Father and the Lord Jesus Christ."

1:3–11 Prayer for the Philippians

Following the salutation, Paul offers his prayer in behalf of the Philippians. The prayer is divided into two sections. First comes a word of thanksgiving growing out of his deep and abiding love for the readers and for their participation in the work of the gospel (1:3–8). At the heart of his passion is the conviction that God is at work in their midst and will be until the day of Christ. Although the wish for health often appeared in the opening of letters in the ancient world, thanks to

---

New Testament Studies held at Christ Church, Oxford, 1965 (ed. F. L. Cross; 2 vols.; TUGAL 102–3; Berlin: Akademie-Verlag, 1968), 371–76. The problem with Best's position is that it is far too subtle. It hangs on an understanding of the preposition *syn* as exclusive (the basis for drawing a distinction between "all the saints" and the "bishops and deacons") rather than Paul's more customary usage of *syn* as inclusive. That his readers would detect the "irony" seems remote.

7. Meeks, *First Urban Christians*, 131–36.

8. Karl Barth et al., *The Epistle to the Philippians* (40th anniversary ed.; Louisville, Ky.: Westminster John Knox, 2002), 12.

a god was seldom expressed, and when it was used, it became a way for the writer to indicate that he was doing well at the time of writing.[9] Paul, who regularly includes a prayer of thanksgiving at the opening of his letters, does not thank God here for his deliverance from danger but rather for his readers' participation in the gospel. The second section contains the matters about which he intercedes for them: that their love may overflow with knowledge and perception, to enable them to discern what really makes a difference in this life (1:9–11).

> 1:3 I give thanks to my God at every remembrance of you,[a] 4 always in my every prayer in behalf of all of you, making my prayer with joy. 5 I thank God for your partnership in the gospel from the first day until now. 6 I am confident of this very thing: that the one who began among you a good work will bring it to completion at the day of Christ Jesus. 7 Just as it is right for me to think this about you all because you[b] hold me in your heart, both in my imprisonment and in the defense and confirmation of the gospel, because all of you are participants with me in this grace. 8 For God is my witness how I yearn for you all with the compassion of Christ Jesus. 9 And this I am praying: that your love may increase more and more, with knowledge and all insight; 10 that you may discern what really matters, in order that you may be genuine and without blame at the day of Christ, 11 having been filled with the fruit of righteousness that comes through Jesus Christ for the glory and praise of God.[c]

a. As a genitive, the "you" could refer to the readers' remembrance of Paul ("at your every remembrance [of me]";[10] though without the "of me" in the Greek, the sentence makes better sense as Paul's remembrance of the readers rather than the readers' remembrance of Paul. Normally verbs of remembering are followed by a genitive of the one or ones remembered (cf. Rom 1:8; 1 Thess 1:7; Phlm 7).

b. Grammatically, one could make as good a case for rendering this clause "I have you in my heart" (NIV) as for "you hold me in your heart" (NRSV). The context, however, supports the translation "you hold me in your heart." Paul explains why it is right for him to think so positively of the Philippians. They have not forgotten him, but have become participants with him in the spread of the gospel.

c. One early manuscript (P^{46}) reads "to the glory of God and my praise." Hooker speculates that the reading is so unusual that it may be the original.[11] However, since Jewish prayers normally end with the phrase "to the glory of God" and since there is no comparable expression elsewhere in Paul's letters to "my praise," it seems wise to take the shorter reading.

---

9. John L. White, *The Apostle of God: Paul and the Promise of Abraham* (Peabody, Mass.: Hendrickson, 1999), 68–69.
10. So O'Brien, *Philippians*, 56–61.
11. Hooker, "Philippians," 486.

Generally the prayers of thanksgiving in the Pauline letters are rhetorically intended to accomplish two functions: (a) to establish rapport with the readers, and (b) to introduce significant themes that will recur in the letter. The former function is not difficult to do in Philippians since Paul expresses his delight in their "sharing in the gospel from the first day until now" (1:5). The warmth and the intimacy that Paul feels toward his readers are genuinely expressed.

The second function is clear in Philippians as well. Years ago Paul Schubert[12] indicated how the prayer at the beginning serves to telegraph the major themes that appear later in the letter, such as:

- joy—1:4, 18, 25; 2:2, 17–18, 28, 29; 3:1; 4:1, 4, 10
- sharing/participation (*koinōnia* and derivatives)—1:5, 7; 2:1; 3:10; 4:14, 15
- gospel—1:5, 7, 12, 16, 27; 2:22; 4:3, 15
- thinking/mind (*phronein* and derivatives)—1:7; 2:2, 5; 3:15, 19; 4:2, 8, 10
- imprisonment—1:7, 12–14, 19–26, 30; 4:14
- compassion/love—1:8, 9, 16; 2:1–2, 12; 4:1
- all—1:4, 7, 8, 25; 2:17, 26; 4:21
- future eschatological references—1:6, 10; 2:16; 3:11–12, 20–21

These themes certainly pick up the major motifs of the letter.

Paul tends to use "all" quite often in prayers of thanksgiving, though the nine uses of *pas* and its derivatives in the opening to the Philippians letter are unusual. Most of the occasions seem to stress the inclusiveness of the readers—"to all the saints" (1:1); "in behalf of you all" (1:4); "concerning all of you" (1:7); "for all of you" (1:8). This has led some commentators to go a step further and to contend that the frequent use of *pas* (what Lightfoot called "a studied repetition"[13]) exposes disunity within the congregation that the apostle is addressing right from the beginning.[14] However, such a conclusion overlooks the fact that many of the uses of *pas* have to do with Paul's persistence in praying and not with the situation of the readers—"every remembrance of you" (1:3); "always" (1:4). The fact that the first eleven verses are replete with commendations of the Philippians makes unlikely the case for serious disunity in the congregation.

1:3–8 Thanksgiving

Three activities are mentioned as reasons for Paul's thanksgiving. First, that the Philippians have "shared in the gospel" no doubt reflects their gifts to him to

---

12. Paul Schubert, *Form and Function of the Pauline Thanksgiving* (Berlin: Töpelmann, 1939), 77.
13. Lightfoot, *Philippians*, 81–83.
14. Peterlin, *Disunity*, 19–30.

undergird his ministry, the most recent of which was carried by Epaphroditus (4:10–20). But more than merely monetary support, Paul is thankful that Euodia, Syntyche, and Clement, among others, have been co-workers, struggling side by side with him in the work of the gospel (4:3–4). The missionary outreach of the community has been an occasion for great joy.

Second, Paul is thankful not only for the Philippians and what they have done, but for God's activity in their midst. His confidence in God's reliable work is particularly appropriate in light of the current (or impending) suffering the readers will undergo (1:27–30). They and Paul can be buoyed by the fact that "the one who has begun among you a good work will carry it to completion at the day of Jesus Christ" (1:6).

Third, Paul can give thanks to God for the mutuality and intimacy that exist between the Philippians and himself. They hold him in their hearts, even in his imprisonment, and he uses an unusual and potent expression in saying that he yearns for them "with the compassion [*en splanchnois*, literally, "the bowels"] of Jesus Christ" (v. 8). Paul describes his own situation as facing a "defense [*apologia*] and confirmation [*bebaiōsis*] of the gospel" (v. 7). Both Greek words have legal connotations and seem to depict the apostle's upcoming trial. The Philippians remember him in their prayers to the end that his preaching will be faithful and that his performance at his trial will be the kind of witness that confirms and validates the gospel.

One can sum up these three features with the term *koinōnia* and its cognates (1:5, 7), a term that is often weakened by translating it as "fellowship." Clearly in this letter it has more of the notions of participation, identification, and involvement. The Philippians have supported Paul by their prayers, by their gifts, and by participation in the mission of the gospel. It is interesting to observe, in a letter serving as an expression of thanks for gifts received, that of the six uses of *koinōnia* and its cognates, several do not include a monetary element (2:1; 3:10) but designate a connection with the Spirit or with Jesus Christ. This makes for a three-way relationship between Paul, the Philippians, and Jesus Christ.

These three features also provide a basis for the joy that Paul expresses, even though he is in prison. The noun "joy" and its cognate verbs appear fourteen times in the letter. That the Philippians have joined him in the cause of the gospel and that with confidence he can rely on God to complete what has been begun in their midst give him reason to rejoice and to invite them to rejoice with him (2:17–18; 4:4). He can even rejoice when the gospel is preached by those with less than genuine motivations (1:15–18).

What precisely is the "good work" that God has initiated in or among the Philippians and that God will complete (1:6)? Is it the salvation of the readers that Paul has in mind?[15] Or is the "good work" the activity in which the Philippians

---

15. O'Brien, *Philippians*, 64.

have become engaged with Paul? The two, of course, need not be mutually exclusive, and yet there is a strong sense of mission in the letter. The readers are told to hold out to the world the word of life and to live as innocent and blameless children of God "in the midst of a crooked and perverse generation, in which you shine like stars in the world" (2:15). The end of God's activity, then, is not merely the salvation of the individual Philippian Christians, but their continued engagement in the gospel, a mission that can be completed only as the readers maintain unity in the face of opposition (1:27–30; cf. also 1 Thess 1:6–10).[16]

The word "day" appears three times in the prayer (1:5, 6, 10), twice in the expression "the day of Jesus Christ." The latter two uses reflect an eschatological symbol that goes back as far as the time of Amos. The prophet warns a presumptuous Israel that when "the day of the Lord" comes, it can turn out to be darkness and not light, "gloom with no brightness in it" (Amos 5:18–20). In the prayer, "day" occurs in two ways. The initial reception of the gospel is designated as "the first day" (1:5). Hearing the word of divine grace and sharing with others its power is like Eden all over again, the creation of something entirely new. But the "day of Jesus Christ" is the final day, the day of Jesus' return, when the veil will be removed and the good beginnings will be completed.

Appropriately this passage (1:3–11) appears as the designated reading in the Common Lectionary for the second Sunday in Advent. The eschatological language of the text provides a dynamic framework in which to reflect on God's activity and on the demands laid on the Christian community. The church lives between the two days. On the one hand, "the first day" signifies the hearing and sharing of the gospel, which has called the community into being. It represents something entirely new, the beginning of life. To be sure, there are moral ambiguities as well as fierce opposition to be faced, because the world in which the church lives is yet unfulfilled. The "day of Jesus Christ" remains in the future. On the other hand, the church lives expectantly, awaiting the "day of Jesus Christ" in the confidence that the God who has begun a good work will bring it to fruition.

1:9–11 Petition

In the light of this situation, Paul's intercessions in behalf of the Philippian community are appropriate (1:9–11). He prays that their love increase more and more

---

16. So Hawthorne, *Philippians*, 21. The noun for "gospel" (*euangelion*) appears in Phil eight times. In none of these instances is there a particular stress on the content of the "gospel" (as in 1 Cor 15:1–11), nor is it pitted over against another message (as in Gal 1:6–7). It rather seems to designate the mission, the cause in which Paul and the Philippians are engaged. It is something that can be "advanced" (1:16). In 4:15 "the beginning of the gospel" connotes the beginning of the mission in Macedonia. It is clear that an itinerant evangelist, whose primary concern was the spread and movement of the gospel, wrote this letter.

with knowledge and full insight, that they develop the capacity to distinguish what is important from what is trivial, that they be genuine and blameless at the day of Christ, and that they produce a harvest of righteousness that ultimately glorifies God. Each of the four petitions has about it an air of exhortation and in a sense prepares the way for other injunctions that follow in the letter.

Not surprising is the petition that the Philippians' love abound; it is the thrust of the exhortation found in 1:27–2:18. But that their love abound in full knowledge (or recognition) and depth of insight (or discrimination) is distinctive. Paul is essentially pointing to the moral character of love, as over against a self-indulgent love that is indiscriminate or impulsive or thoroughly turned in on itself.

Discernment becomes a critical ingredient in the Christian experience for Paul. It is the result of being transformed by the renewal of the mind, "so that you may discern what is the will of God—what is good and acceptable and perfect" (Rom 12:2). To discern is not only to distinguish right from wrong, but also to sort out the good from the not-so-good, the valuable from the worthless, the significant from the trivial.[17]

The intent of such discernment is threefold. First, the Philippians are to be genuine and without blame at the day of Christ. The meaning of the Greek word for "genuine" (*eilikrinēs*) may or may not have derived from its etymology "tested by the light of the sun," but it has come to designate someone sincere, without hidden motives or pretense. It is appropriately joined with the adjective "blameless," or better, "giving no cause for offense" (cf. 1 Cor 10:32; Acts 24:16; 1 Pet 1:17).[18] Paul calls for a love that is genuine and that in no way can be deemed counterfeit or heedlessly harmful to the neighbor (cf. Rom 12:9).

Finally, since Paul appreciates the Philippians as genuine and blameless and observes that, for them, the fruit of righteousness is ultimately for "the glory and praise of God" (1:11), it is fitting that the prayer for the Philippians should conclude with a doxology. Failure to acknowledge God entails the loss of the glory [*doxa*] of God (Rom 3:23); however, God, both the source and goal of life (Phil 3:20–21), graciously restores the divine glory (Rom 5:2) and thus is worthy of all human praise. "Glory" entails more than fame and reputation. In the Hebrew Scriptures, it is one of God's attributes; it characterizes God's unique being, mirrored in the heavens (Ps 19:1; Hab 3:3) and pervading the earth (Isa 6:3). The one who has begun a good work among the Philippians (1:6) will surely answer the apostle's prayers in regard to his "defense and confirmation of the gospel" and their growth in perception and insight.

17. J. Paul Sampley, *Walking between the Times: Paul's Moral Reasoning* (Minneapolis: Fortress, 1991), 53–56, 81–83.

18. Friedrich Büchsel, "εἰλικρινής, εἰλικρίνεα," *TDNT*, 2:397; Walter Bauer and Frederick W. Danker, eds., *A Greek-English Lexicon of the New Testament and Other Early Christian Literature* (trans. Frederick W. Danker and William Arndt; 3d ed.; Chicago: University of Chicago Press, 2000), 282.

1:12–26 Reassurance about the Sender

Paul is in jail and has much about which to complain. His efforts to spread the gospel have been complicated by a group, apparently envious of him, whose members delight in undermining his own work. They preach the same gospel, but do it out of "selfish ambition," not genuinely, but in a deliberate attempt to make life harder on the apostle. There are also no doubt many who take his imprisonment as an indication that the gospel has failed. While there is no hint that his apostleship is being challenged, there are those whose enthusiasm would be dampened by learning of the incarceration of the leader of this new faith. Furthermore, Paul always has hanging over him his own trial. Will he be freed, or will he be killed? In one sense he is at the mercy of his Roman captors. In another sense, he feels that God still has work for him to do. And yet in spite of all the reasons he has to complain, Paul "rejoices" (1:18).

Our task in reading this section of the letter will be to diagnose what transpires for the apostle and to determine why his report of his situation is as positive as it is. It is important that we hunt for the theological reasons for his optimism and not revert to a psychological explanation. While he uses the first-person pronoun frequently, we simply do not have the personal data necessary for the latter, while what he reports is heavily theological in character.

The section 1:12–26 is divided into three brief paragraphs:

- Paul's imprisonment and the progress of the gospel (1:12–14)
- Two contrasting types of preachers of the gospel (1:15–18a)
- Paul's immediate future and the progress of the gospel (1:18b–26)

What is highly significant is that the Greek noun *prokope*, meaning "progress" or "advancement," appears in 1:12 and 1:25 and forms an *inclusio* around the section. Paul's report on his situation in prison turns out to be an account of the growth and spread of the Christian message.

1:12–14 Paul's Imprisonment and the Spread of the Gospel

1:12 I want you to know, brothers and sisters,[a] that the things that have happened to me have turned out instead[b] for the advancement of the gospel. 13 As a result, it has become obvious among the whole imperial guard[c] and all the rest that my imprisonment is in Christ[d] and 14 that most of the brothers and sisters, having been made confident in the Lord[e] by my imprisonment, dare to speak the word[f] so much more fearlessly.

a. The NRSV rending of *adelphoi* as "beloved" unfortunately loses the family connotation of the term.

Reassurance about the Sender

b. *Mallon* is better rendered as "instead" or "rather" and not as "more" or "to a greater degree."

c. *Praitōrion* clearly refers to imperial soldiers and not to a place (such as a headquarters or barracks), since it is parallel to "all the rest."

d. Most translations read "for Christ"; however, the preposition is *en* and would seem to imply that what has become known is that Paul's suffering is a sharing in Christ's suffering. The prepositional phrase would then indicate that his incarceration was not simply the result of his preaching of Christ, but a means of proclaiming it.[1]

e. The phrase "in the Lord" could be understood as modifying "brothers and sisters," but this would seem superfluous since "brothers and sisters" refers to believers. Thus "in the Lord" is better taken with "having been made confident."

f. Some ancient and trustworthy manuscripts (Codices Sinaiticus, Alexandrinus, and Vaticanus) add "of God" or "of the Lord" to clarify what "word" was being spoken. While their interpretation is no doubt correct, it is probably best to choose the shorter reading, which then in turn explains the origin of the other readings.

[1:12—14] Paul begins with what is called a "disclosure formula" ("I want you to know") and the familiar direct address ("brothers and sisters"), which is typical of the way he moves to the bodies of letters (so Rom 1:13; 2 Cor 1:8; Gal 1:11; 1 Thess 2:1). It signals a shift from the introductory prayer to the business at hand, which in Philippians is a report on his situation in prison. The section that follows (1:12–26) is rather lengthy. Not even Philemon, which was also written from prison, contains such a detailed statement of his personal circumstances. Why? It may be due to the fact that Paul wants to relieve the anxieties that the Philippians have about his plight and his upcoming trial, or it may be due to the suspicions of some of his readers that his imprisonment symbolizes the failure of the gospel. The latter would seem more likely in light of the emphasis Paul puts on the "advancement of the gospel" (1:12, 25).

Paul uses the term "the advancement of the gospel" to depict an extended preaching of the gospel in two ways. First, the gospel is extended because it has become clear among the whole imperial guard and "all the rest" that Paul's imprisonment is "in Christ." Though most translations read "for Christ" (1:13), the customary rendering of *en Christō* makes better sense despite its awkwardness. What his Roman captors have come to see is that the sufferings he endures because of his imprisonment unite Paul with the sufferings of Christ (see 3:10). Thus his incarceration has become a means for the progress of the gospel.

Second, Paul's imprisonment has made his brothers and sisters more daring in their own proclamation of the gospel. They have grown fearless, apparently unintimidated by those in the imperial guard who fail to see Paul's being in chains as a witness to Christ. These colleagues have developed a renewed enthusiasm for the faith, and they draw strength from the apostle's plight. In the

---

1. See Hooker, "Philippians," 488.

midst of the first century, with Nero growing in power and increasingly hostile to Christians,[2] Paul's contagious exuberance encourages his brothers and sisters to practice the gospel with boldness. O'Brien calls attention to the accumulation of terms in 1:14 that express their courage—*pepoithotas* ("having been made confident"), *perissoterōs* ("so much more"), *tolmaō* ("dare"), and *aphobōs* ("fearlessly").[3]

Paul has repeatedly used the term "gospel" (*euangelion*), and we need to pause and examine its significance. It occurs six times in chapter 1 of Philippians and, with one exception ("the gospel of Christ," in 1:27), without any explanatory phrase. (Undoubtedly "the word" in 1:14 is also to be read as a synonym to "the gospel.") Two observations are to be made about the use of "gospel" in Philippians. First, no description of the word is offered, and thus it must have been familiar to the readers, something in fact that Paul shared with them. Margaret Mitchell comments, "Paul's punctuated abbreviations unite his readers with himself and one another in a common bond of shared language and assumptions, a task central to the formation of ecclesial self-identity and social cohesion."[4] "Gospel" is one of those extremely packed abbreviations that serve to cultivate a sense of mutuality and belonging on the part of the readers. It carries with it emotional weight as well as being a statement of the good news of what God has done in the death and resurrection of Jesus.

Second, Graham Stanton argues convincingly that there is a political background against which early Christians would hear and use the term "gospel."[5] As a singular noun (as it always appears in the Pauline letters, *euangelion*), it would be differentiated from the rival "gospels" of the imperial cult (where the word customarily appears in the plural, *euangelia*). First-century propaganda contended that providence would not provide a better savior than Augustus, the supreme benefactor, son of God, who brought peace to a strife-ridden world.[6]

---

2. For example, Tacitus writes, "First . . . the confessed members of the [Christian] sect were arrested; next, on their disclosures vast numbers were convicted . . . for their hatred of the human race. And derision accompanied their end: they were covered in wild beasts' skins and torn apart by dogs; or they were fastened on crosses, and when daylight failed, were burned to serve as lamps by night" (Tacitus, *The Annals of Tacitus* [trans. John Jackson; Cambridge, Mass.: Harvard University Press, 1937], 2:15).

3. O'Brien, *Philippians*, 94.

4. Margaret M. Mitchell, "Rhetorical Shorthand in Pauline Argumentation: The Function of the Gospel in the Corinthian Correspondence," in *Gospel in Paul: Studies on Corinthians, Galatians and Romans for Richard N. Longenecker* (ed. L. Ann Jervis and Peter Richardson; JSNTSup 108; Sheffield: Sheffield Academic Press, 1994), 88.

5. Graham Stanton, *Jesus and Gospel* (Cambridge: Cambridge University Press, 2004), 47–52.

6. According to Tacitus, "At home, all was calm. . . . All eyes looked to the mandate of the sovereign—with no immediate misgivings, so long as Augustus in the full vigour of his prime upheld himself, his house, and peace" (Tacitus, *Annales*, 1:3–4).

Reassurance about the Sender

Over against the all-pervasive cult of the empire is spoken this "gospel," whose message of God's redeeming act in Christ subverts the work of savior Augustus and those who follow in his train. Stanton goes on to warn that of all the words and phrases used to depict God's good news, "only the gospel word has verbal links with the language of the imperial cult." Hence one must be "wary of assuming that with every early Christian use of this word group the imperial cult is lurking in the background."[7]

Given that Philippi is a Roman colony populated by a number of retired military personnel, Paul's declaration that the gospel has "advanced" (1:12, 25) in the face of his imprisonment provides an encouraging (if subversive) report, to say the least. That it has infiltrated the imperial guard, in that they understand why Paul suffers, is an even more positive word for his readers to hear. "Gospel" is the reality that binds the community together and in which both Paul and the Philippians share (1:5, 7). It provides an ecclesial identity for the community and even enables the apostle to accept those preachers whose motives are less than genuine. The gospel's "progress," then, is an occasion for rejoicing.

1:15–18a Contrasting Preachers of the Gospel

15 Some, on the one hand, preach Christ out of envy and rivalry; others, on the other hand, because of the divine will.[a] 16 Some do so out of love, knowing that I am put here for the defense of the gospel. 17 Others preach Christ out of selfish ambition, not genuinely, but rather thinking they can stir up trouble for me while I am in jail. 18 But what does it matter? Only that in every way, whether in pretense or in truth, Christ is being proclaimed; and in this I am rejoicing.

a. The Greek word *eudokia* can be translated as "goodwill," implying the attitude of the preachers toward Paul (NRSV). The fact, however, that the preposition is *dia*, with the accusative of *eudokia*, leads toward understanding *eudokia* as the cause of their preaching, namely, the divine will.

[1:15–18a] This brief section contrasts two types of preachers of the gospel. Three literary features heighten the disparity. First, the *men . . . de* ("on the one hand . . . on the other hand") in 1:15–17a clearly distinguishes the two groups from one another. The fact that the sentence structure is repeated simply underlines the contrast. Second, the presentation takes the form of a forceful chiasm (A, B, B', A'):

---

7. Stanton, *Jesus*, 61.

   A Some preach Christ from envy and rivalry (1:15)
   B Others because of the divine will (1:15)
   B' These out of love, knowing that I am put here for the defense of the gospel (1:16)
   A' Others out of selfish ambition, not genuinely, thinking they can stir up trouble for me while I am in jail (1:17).

A third feature that underlines the distinction is the intriguing use of the two participles "knowing" (*eidotes*) and "thinking" or "imagining" (*oiomenoi*). The one group "knows" that Paul's vocation is to defend the gospel; the other group only "imagines" that they can stir up trouble for him in his imprisonment.

Two questions arise concerning these two groups of preachers. Who are they, and why does Paul take such a generous stance toward those preaching from base motives? They are apparently Christians, yet they seek to make Paul's life in prison more difficult. Envy, rivalry, and strife are characteristic of their attitude toward the apostle. Is it simply a personal animosity they have toward Paul, or does the tension have to do with their anti-imperial politics?[8] Frankly, the terms Paul uses to depict this group are so general that it is impossible to identify exactly what motivates the group.[9] We are left with two ill-defined groups of preachers, one acting out of love, and the other acting from a spirit of competition.

In any case, Paul shows remarkable generosity toward the second cluster of preachers. (Contrast this with his uncompromising attitude toward the agitators in Galatia—"I wish those who unsettle you would castrate themselves!"[10]) He writes, "What does it matter? Only that in every way, whether in pretense or in truth, Christ is being preached, and in that I am rejoicing" (v. 18). Paul's indifference toward the ill will they bear toward him is astonishing. They preach the gospel, and that seems to be all that matters. As Schütz comments, "The motives of the proclamation of the gospel are subordinated to the fact of its proclamation and then regarded as secondary."[11] What we have is the supremacy of the message over the ambitions of the preachers of the message.

Paul's report of his situation to the Philippians has as yet said nothing regarding his trial and what he anticipates occurring. He has been preoccupied with the advancement of the gospel and with its infiltration even among the imperial guard. That has given him cause for rejoicing. Now it is time to reflect on his personal situation, his premonitions regarding his trial, and whether he expects to be released or to be killed. While Paul can discuss his future in the

    8. For a survey of proposals, see O'Brien, *Philippians*, 100–105.
    9. See Introduction p. 15 for further comments on the two types of preachers mentioned in 1:15–17.
    10. Gal 5:12, cf: 1:6–9; 3:1–3; 4:19–21; 5:1–4.
    11. John Howard Schütz, *Paul and the Anatomy of Apostolic Authority* (with new introduction by Wayne Meeks, ed.; NTL; Louisville, Ky.: Westminster John Knox, 2007), 161.

Reassurance about the Sender

context of joy (1:18), his readers are no doubt uneasy and even threatened at the prospect of his death since his relationship with them has been so close and intimate. Thus the apostle writes with care.

1:18b–26 Paul's Anticipated Deliverance

1:18b Indeed also I shall continue to rejoice, **19** for I know that this will turn out for my deliverance[a] through your prayers and the support of the Spirit of Jesus Christ. **20** It is my eager anticipation and hope that in no way will I be ashamed, but with all frankness[b] of speech Christ will be exalted now and always in my body,[c] whether I live or I die. **21** For me to live is Christ and to die is gain. **22** If I am to live in the flesh, this will mean fruitful labor for me; and I do not know which I prefer.[d] **23** I am torn between the two: having the desire to depart and to be with Christ, which is far, far better; **24** but to remain in the flesh is more necessary for you. **25** I am confident of this: I know that I will remain and will continue with you all for your progress and joy of the faith. **26** This way I share abundantly in your boasting in Christ Jesus by coming again to you.

    a. The Greek word *sōtēria* can denote a historical deliverance of some sort or eschatological salvation. In this context, Paul is probably thinking not merely of his release from jail or of eternal salvation, but of God's vindication of his stand for the gospel. This is likely because the text echoes Job 13:16.

    b. The Greek word *parrēsia* implies speech that is open to public scrutiny and includes a candor that comes "to be seen as a touchstone for discriminating the true friend from the self-serving toady."[12]

    c. Though the customary Greek word for "body" is used (*sōma*), it clearly refers to the whole person, "the instrument of human experience and suffering."[13]

    d. Some translations render the verb as "choose" (NIV), others as "prefer" (NRSV). Both are proper renderings of the Greek verb; however, it is hard to see how Paul would have had any choice in the outcome of his trial. Given the rhetorical trope being used, "prefer" makes better sense.

[1:18b–20] Paul's reflections are aided in 1:19 by a faint echo from the Septuagint of Job 13:16: "Even this will turn out for my deliverance, for deceit shall not enter in before him." Readers familiar with the Septuagint can hear in the words of Paul an association with the righteous sufferer, Job, who rebuts the thesis of one of his comforters that his troubles are the result of divine punishment for his evil ways. As Job expresses confidence that he will be delivered from his

---

    12. David Konstans, "Friendship, Frankness, and Flattery," in *Friendship, Flattery, and Frankness of Speech: Studies on Friendship in the New Testament World* (ed. John T. Fitzgerald; NovTSup 82; Leiden: Brill, 1996), 12.

    13. Bauer and Danker, eds., BDAG, 983.

trials, so Paul affirms that, however the trial turns out, God will confirm his defense of the gospel.[14] This suggests further that the "deliverance" (*sōtēria*) claimed in 1:19 is neither release from prison nor eschatological salvation, but God's vindication of Paul's "defense and confirmation of the gospel" (1:7, 16). In this, the prayers of the Philippians and the ample supply of the spirit support him.

The words "eager expectation" and "hope" are two terms Paul links elsewhere (Rom 8:19–20, 23–24), which express for him more than a personal desire that the outcome will turn out in a particular way. As Bockmuehl puts it, "Hope in the Bible is based on the fact that God is God and has underwritten the future. In keeping with this understanding of hope (and contrary to certain alternative interpretations), Paul's 'eager expectation' is therefore a confident rather than an anxious disposition."[15]

Paul nevertheless expects to have a voice in his trial. His hope is that he will not be shamed in the process but that he will be able to speak with "boldness" so that Christ will be magnified or praised in his experience. However the verdict goes, his critical concern is faithfulness. The urgency that surrounds the trial for the apostle is not whether he will lose the case and thus lose his life, but whether he will be given *parrēsia*, bold and frank speech, to speak the gospel. Only with such bold speech is Christ honored in Paul's person.

[1:21–24] Not only is Paul motivated by a sure hope in God, but his reflections on death and life are bound up with the theme of rejoicing (1:18b, 25). Though the apostle's statement that "to depart and be with Christ is far better" (v. 23) has been interpreted by some as a suicide wish[16] or at least as a desire to be released from his present burdens,[17] the context prevents one from interpreting Paul as a depressed person seeking death. The emphases on hope and joy simply do not mesh with a suicidal tendency or with the notion that his present sufferings are more than he can handle.

The apostle does, however, reflect on the meaning of living and dying. He does so by using an alternating pattern, which certainly enhances the rhetorical effect of the section.

a. To live is Christ (1:21a).
b. To die is gain (1:21b).
c. Living in the flesh means fruitful labor (1:22).
d. To depart and to be with Christ is far better (1:23).
e. To remain in the flesh is more necessary for you (1:24).

---

14. Richard B. Hays, *Echoes of Scripture in the Letters of Paul* (New Haven, Conn.: Yale University Press, 1989), 21–24.
15. Bockmuehl, *Philippians*, 84.
16. So J. Arthur Droge, "Mori Lucrum: Paul and Ancient Theories of Suicide," *NovT* 30 (1988): 63–86.
17. So D. W. Palmer, "To Die Is Gain (Phil 1:21)," *NovT* 17 (1975): 203–18.

Paul appears confident that he will be released from prison, but he nevertheless faces the prospect that the verdict might go against him. He apparently will have no choice in the matter. It will not be his decision. But which alternative would he prefer? To live is Christ. That means "knowing the power of his resurrection and participating in his sufferings" (3:10); it means living out a righteousness that is not one's own, but is a righteousness received by the faith of Christ (3:9); it means "fruitful labor" (1:22); it means continued involvement with the Philippians for their advancement and joy in the faith (1:25). To die is gain, and in a sense that is far better. Death makes possible an enlargement of the experience of Christ. But Paul does not linger over the prospect of dying, for he is confident that he will live and will remain with the Philippians (1:25).

What Paul is likely doing in 1:19–24 is employing a rhetorical trope, known as "feigned perplexity" (Greek: *aporia* and *diaporēsis*; Latin: *dubitatio* and *addubitatio*). N. Clayton Croy calls attention to the technique of pretending uncertainty and posing a question as a way of strengthening one's argument.[18] Cicero provides an explanation and an example. "Indecision occurs when the speaker seems to ask which of two or more words he had better use, as follows: 'At that time the republic suffered exceedingly from—ought I to say—the folly of the consuls, or their wickedness, or both.'"[19]

In Paul's own mind he knows that he will live and will work again with the Philippians (which he gets around to acknowledging finally in 1:25–26). Meanwhile he is hard-pressed between the alternatives of living and dying. His playing of one off against the other and his rejection of departing and "being with Christ" result in a subtle invitation to others to follow the apostle's example. Plus, Paul provides a dramatic conclusion to his pledge of commitment, by utilizing the "feigned perplexity" trope.

This passage raises a notoriously difficult issue regarding Paul's eschatology. In writing 1 Thessalonians the apostle seems to anticipate being alive himself at the return of Jesus (1 Thess 4:15), and in 1 Corinthians he declares that believers who die remain in an intermediate state of sleep until Christ returns, when they will be transformed and clothed with immortality (1 Cor 15:35–55; 1 Thess 4:13–5:10). But here in Philippians, he speaks of departing and being with Christ now (1:23) and of dying as being "gain" (1:21). How do we reconcile the two eschatological postures?

Some scholars argue that Paul has made a change in his perspective from an earlier time when he anticipated being alive at the return of Christ until a later time when he had come to grips with his own death. This argument represents a natural reading in light of the delay of the Parousia. But an explanation that

---

18. N. Clayton Croy, "'To Die Is Gain,' Philippians 1:19–26: Does Paul Contemplate Suicide?" *JBL* 122 (2002): 517–30.

19. *Rhetorica ad Herennium* 4.30; cited by Croy, "'To Die Is Gain,'" 526.

entails an evolution of Paul's thought assumes that the letters were written in a certain order (and obviously that Philippians came late). It also ignores other verses in Philippians that anticipate a future consummation in the relatively near future (1:6, 10; 2:16; 3:11, 14, 20–21). As to the order in which the letters were written, Philippians may be the last or it may come in the mid-50s parallel to the Corinthian correspondence.[20]

Three other suggestions offer a solution to the eschatological dilemma. First, Barth contends that the matter of life beyond death is actually secondary to the text and that the "gain" (which is "being with Christ") refers to Paul's death itself. If Christ is magnified "in his body" by death (1:22), this surely is "the final consummate act" (so 3:10), bringing a closer identification with Christ than is possible in life and thus a "gain."[21] Barth closely follows Lohmeyer, who interprets the entire letter as a reflection on martyrdom. In this passage Paul muses on the potentiality of being a martyr himself and thus, at his death, being fully with Christ, something that for ordinary believers will come only at the return of Christ.[22] The difficulty with the proposal of Barth and Lohmeyer is its tendency to exalt martyrdom to such a high position that Paul becomes isolated from his fellow believers in Philippi. Often the apostle acknowledges his connection with his readers (1:30), but his call to them to imitate him (3:17) does not reflect a passionate lust for martyrdom as one finds later in Ignatius ("To the Romans," 4:1–3).

Second, Caird suggests that Paul is drawing on the metaphor of sleep, which he frequently uses as analogous to death (1 Cor 7:39; 11:30; 15:6, 15, 20, 51; 1 Thess 4:13–15). Sleep negates the passage of time so that the first thing a person is aware of is the consciousness of waking up. When believers fall asleep in death (i.e., depart and be with Christ), their next conscious awareness is the day of Christ's return. A person passes into the presence of God at death, which becomes simultaneously the return of Christ. Thus Phil 1:21–24 represents no change in eschatology from an earlier period, but a solution to the problem of the relation of time and eternity.[23] The difficulty with Caird's position is that Paul does not employ the metaphor of sleep at all in Philippians, and we have no indication that these readers would have had access to Corinthians or Thessalonians. Thus, one can hardly assume that they had knowledge of the metaphor, at least as Paul has used it elsewhere.

A third (and the most likely) interpretation does not contradict the notion in Corinthians and Thessalonians that believers who die remain in an intermedi-

---

20. The dating of the letter is of course connected to the place of Paul's imprisonment. For a full discussion, see Introduction, pp. 9–11.
21. Barth et al., *Philippians*, 38–42.
22. Lohmeyer, *Briefe*, 59–70.
23. G. B. Caird, *Paul's Letters from Prison: Ephesians, Philippians, Colossians, Philemon: In the Revised Standard Version* (NCIB; London: Oxford University Press, 1976), 112–14.

ate state[24] until the return of Christ, but contends that what is being said in 1:21–23 involves an enriching of the relationship with Christ, not a break in it (cf. 2 Cor 5:6–8). Death for believers brings a deeper union with Christ, and thus is "gain" (1:21), and yet it is not synonymous with the return of Christ. Lincoln concludes, "It is clear from a comparison of Phil 1:23 with 3:20, 21 that the state into which Paul will enter at death is far better, bringing with it a greater closeness of communion with Christ, and yet it is still a state of expectation, less than the fullness of redemption described in 3:20f."[25]

[25–26] Despite the uncertainties voiced in 1:21–24, the paragraph ends on a positive note. Paul delights in his readers' ministry and seems convinced that he will join them and share in their "progress and joy in the faith" (v. 25). Though he prefers the "gain" that being fully with Christ would bring, his involvement with the Philippians is not a poor, second choice. This becomes obvious in Paul's play on the words *epimenō* (1:24), and *menō* and *paramenō* (1:25). "Remaining in the flesh" means "staying" with the Philippians and "continuing" for their progress and joy in the faith.

This is all to the end that, literally, "your cause for boasting might abound in Christ Jesus in me through my coming again to you" (1:26). The NRSV softens the verse by reading "that I may share abundantly in your boasting in Christ Jesus when I come to you again," whereas the NIV renders the verse "so that through my being with you again your joy in Christ Jesus will overflow on account of me." Each seems to be trying to prevent Paul from sounding arrogant or boastful. The word *kauchēma,* however, means the reason or cause for boasting. He apparently is saying that now in prison he looks forward to being with them at a time when they can glorify God not only because of Christ but also because he is free and able to be with them again. His being with them makes him the cause for boasting.

Paul's report to the Philippians on his whereabouts concludes, then, not in despair or depression because of his confinement in a Roman jail, but with an anticipation of his being present with the Philippians and sharing with them in their growth and joy in the faith. Just as his imprisonment has led to the advancement of the gospel, so Paul is confident of their progress as a body of believers.

---

24. In *The Resurrection of the Son of God* (Minneapolis: Fortress, 2002), N. T. Wright objectifies the language of the resurrection and so has Paul relate two resurrections instead of one. He is working out of an "already–not yet" eschatology, but interprets it in a heavily realized eschatological sense (236–41).

25. Andrew T. Lincoln, *Paradise Now and Not Yet: Studies in the Role of the Heavenly Dimension in Paul's Thought with Special Reference to His Eschatology* (SNTSMS 43; Cambridge: Cambridge University Press, 1981), 106.

1:27–2:18 Concern for the Recipients

Two changes in the cadence of the letter become immediately obvious when one moves from 1:12–26 to 1:27–2:18. The first change is that the focus shifts from Paul and his imprisonment to the situation of the Philippians. Paul no longer reports from his jail cell about how the gospel is progressing, but rather he turns to his readers to offer them encouragement as they face opposition. The second change is a move to the imperative mood (from the indicative). Seven imperatives appear in the section 1:27–2:18. It is as if he uses the words of exhortation to depict what he wants the Philippians to be and to do. These are not harsh imperatives as if Paul is setting straight a recalcitrant group, but are encouraging words, supporting them in their current or upcoming predicament under pressure. The accompanying participles clarify what the imperatives are anticipating.

Four of the imperatives determine the structure of the larger section, composed of four paragraphs:

1. *live as citizens* worthy of the gospel by maintaining unity and courage in the face of the opposition (1:27–30);
2. *make my joy complete* by manifesting a common purpose and by placing the needs of others before your own needs (2:1–4);
3. *let your bearing toward one another arise out of your life in Christ Jesus* (2:5, NEB) so that your humility will be evident in the community (2:5–11);
4. *continue to work out your salvation (i.e., wholeness) in the community*, remembering that God is at work in you, and that you have and are a mission to the world (2:12–18).

1:27–30 To Express Unity and Courage in the Face of Opposition

In letters written in the ancient world, introduction and conclusion both adhere to a precise format. The conventional features so apparent in the openings and closings of letters tend to disappear in the body. When the writer gets down to the real business of communicating what he or she wants to say, there are no strict rules to follow. Alexander observes, however, that in family letters, the writer customarily begins by reporting on his or her own situation, and then seeks assurance from the addressees about their circumstances. If Alexander's proposal is correct, namely, that in writing Philippians Paul follows the pattern of the familial letters, we would anticipate a change from reporting on his whereabouts to an inquiry concerning their situation. This is what Paul seems to do, though he does so in the context of exhortation rather than inquiry.

Concern for the Recipients

Two factors are worthy of note. First, in 1:27 Paul says, "So that, whether I come and see you or am absent and hear about you (*ta peri hymōn*), I will know that you are standing firm in one spirit, striving side by side with one mind for the faith of the gospel, and are in no way intimidated by your opponents" (NRSV). The *ta peri hymōn* closely parallels the expression in 1:12, "what has happened to me" (*ta kat' eme*), which gives the subsections in the Greek more coherence than it may seem in translation. Paul first reports on his own situation and then inquires about his readers.

Second, rather than being solicitous of his readers, Paul describes what he wants to hear about them, namely that they are unified in their stand for the gospel and are not overcome by their opponents. Thus, Alexander's proposal seems on target with regard to Philippians. Paul is eager to learn that the readers are doing well, even in the face of those who are threatened by them and are persecuting them.

The paragraph that begins at 1:27 and continues through 1:30 tells the modern reader a great deal about the situation of the Philippians, namely that they are under pressure, if not persecution, and that their opposition defines their solidarity with the apostle. Paul's words reflect the concern of a pastor and friend.

1:27 Just this one thing[a]: live as citizens[b] worthy of the gospel of Christ, in order that whether I come and see you or am absent and hear of your circumstances, I might know that you are standing firm in one Spirit,[c] striving as one person[d] for the faith of the gospel and **28** that you are not in any way intimidated by those who oppose you. For this is a sign to them of their destruction, but of your deliverance—and this from God.[e] **29** For it has been graciously given to you on behalf of Christ not only to believe on him but also to suffer for his sake, **30** since you are engaged in the same struggle that you saw that I had and now hear that I still have.

a. The neuter of the adjective *monos* ("only") is used, which limits the action of the verb. There is only one thing that matters: that they live lives worthy of the gospel of Christ.

b. "Live your lives" is a bit tame for a translation of *politeuesthe*, a Greek word derivative from the political world (see 3:20) and certainly known to the Philippian readers. It might well be rendered "live as citizens worthy of the gospel of Christ." See the discussion below.

c. The NRSV and the NIV both render *pneuma* as "spirit" with a small "s"; however, in light of 2:1, a good case can be made for the divine Spirit as the reality that unites the community and enables it not to be intimidated by the opposition.[1]

d. The NRSV translates *mia psychē* as "with one mind"; however, Paul is not stressing the mind over against some other human faculty, but calls for the striving as a single individual. Thus "as one person" seems a more appropriate rendering.

---

1. See Ralph P. Martin, *Philippians* (NCB; Grand Rapids: Eerdmans, 1980), 83; Fee, *Philippians,* 163–66.

e. The translation of 1:28b poses several problems. (1) *endeixis* can be rendered "proof," "evidence," "omen," or "sign." I have followed BDAG, in using "sign," though in the ancient world "omen" might suit just as well.[2] (2) Admittedly the grammar of 1:28b is difficult. Hawthorne contends that the verse relates the opponents' attitude toward the Philippians in contrast to what the readers know about themselves ("they see your faithfulness as a sign of your destruction, but you know it to be an indication of your salvation").[3] To arrive at this interpretation, however, Hawthorne has to reconstruct a considerable portion of the verse.

[1:27–28] The appeal to steadfastness is stated in a nuanced fashion that is often lost in translation. The NRSV reads "live your life in a manner worthy of the gospel." The Greek verb used here, however, is not Paul's usual word "walk" (*peripateō*, 1 Thess 2:12; 4:12; Rom 13:13; Gal 5:16; Phil 3:17), which is regularly rendered "conduct oneself" or simply "live," but rather is the imperative of *politeuomai*, which means "to be a citizen of."[4] But how is this "citizenship" to be expressed? There are generally three options. First, Brewer, who has made a thorough study of the uses of the verb in Hellenistic circles, contends that Paul is exhorting the Philippians to be faithful as Christians should be in their civic duties.[5] In a city like Philippi, the admonition could easily be understood as a challenge to readers to take up their responsibilities as citizens of Rome, especially by ensuring that internal disputes do not become public and thereby harm the church's mission. As Winter puts it, "Small private disputes quickly become big matters that spill over into the politeia with debilitating and ongoing consequences for the credibility of the gospel."[6]

Second, most commentators acknowledge the political character of *politeuomai*, but take it metaphorically. They point to 3:20, which states that the Philippians' real citizenship exists in heaven. Yet the apostle is not adding civic responsibilities to their Christian ones as if the gospel demanded loyalty to Rome alongside loyalty to Christ. Rather he reminds them of their loyalty to the gospel and thus to their citizenship in heaven.

Third, a more radical position is taken by Craig Steven de Vos, who interprets 1:27 in light of 3:20.[7] He concludes that when the Philippians read 1:27 as citizens of heaven, they hear a call to renounce their status as Roman citizens and to consider themselves slaves, without rights and privileges within the Roman realm. A life worthy of the gospel implies a surrender of status in the Roman Empire, and renunciation of this magnitude parallels the activity of

---

2. Bauer and Danker, eds., BDAG, 323.
3. Hawthorne, *Philippians*, 58–60.
4. Bauer and Danker, eds., BDAG, 846.
5. R. R. Brewer, "The Meaning of *Politeuesthe* in Philippians 1:27," *JBL* 73 (1954): 76–83.
6. S. C. Winter, "Paul's Letter to Philemon," *NTS* 33 (1987): 1–15.
7. De Vos, *Conflicts*, 282–86.

Christ in the hymn, "who emptied himself, taking on the form of slave" (2:7). This third option has a great deal of appeal, except that it ignores the spread of the gospel among the praetorian guard (1:13) and the concluding greeting that lists among the saints those of Caesar's household (4:22). It would be difficult to think the apostle acknowledges in the same letter both a successful mission among the Roman troops and a call to believers to lay down their Roman citizenship. De Vos's position would be stronger had Paul used his more traditional word "walk," rather than "live as a citizen worthy of the gospel." Thus, the first two options seem the better alternatives. In any case, the Philippians' life is to be determined by the "gospel," which, as we have seen in connection with 1:12–26, connotes always a subversive character.

The apostle specifies two characteristics of a communal life that is worthy of the gospel. One is that the believers stand firm in the one Spirit as a single person, striving hard for the faith of the gospel. This exhortation embraces two metaphors: (1) "Stand firm" (*stēkete*), a military image that portrays soldiers standing in order and not breaking ranks. Individual skills are secondary to the massed unit, with the result that the troops will not turn and run when attacked by enemy forces. Likewise Barth reminds us, "Unity in the Spirit is no task but a gift that people need only to call to mind again in order to be united."[8] (2) "Striving hard" (*synathlountes*), probably an athletic image, denotes a more aggressive stance, like the struggle (*agōna*, 1:30) in which Paul is engaged. The community reflected here is engaged in the work of the gospel. Euodia, Syntyche, Clement, and the others (4:2–3) are later singled out as "fellow workers." The imagery underscores the corporate nature of the struggle in which the Philippians find themselves.

Steadfastness and unity are the first characteristics nourished by the community under attack. Second is an unwillingness to be intimidated by the opposition. Whether by refusal to participate in the imperial cult or unwillingness to acknowledge the authority of Caesar, the Philippians prove themselves a threat to the civic powers. They thereby put themselves at risk. Paul, remarkably, counts the hostility of the political authorities not as an unfortunate turn of events but a sign of grace. The quality of the Philippians' life is so authentic as to bring a negative reaction from the surrounding powers that be. For Paul, this animosity reveals both the demise of the opposition and the "salvation" of the Philippians.

The terms *apōleia* and *sōtēria* are customarily rendered "destruction" and "salvation," yet the apostle does not intend to consign one group to heaven and another to hell. He does not imply that the final judgment is already set. But he does declare that the circumstances in Philippi have lasting consequences, both for those who oppose the believing community and for the community itself.

---

8. Barth et al., *Philippians*, 47.

The Philippians hear this set of circumstances as a word of encouragement and hope, especially when they read that this is God's gift to them. It is not they who have erected this sign in the world, a sign that has eternal significance; it is the gift of God. The statement that "this is from God" leads to an explanation of the divine gift.

[1:29] About 1:29, several features warrant our attention. First, the word order, in which *hymin* ("you") comes first in the sentence following the *hoti* ("for"), is significant. This is not a universal statement that all must suffer, but a pointed word about the readers. Second, the passive verb *echaristhē* (in 1:29, "it has been given") here is a divine passive, in which God is the implied subject. Third, the verb is related to the noun "grace" (*charis*) and carries with it the notion of divine favor. Its other use in Philippians is in 2:9, where God gives to Jesus the name that is above all names. Fourth, the wording of 1:29b closely links "believing" and "suffering" as gifts of God. Faith and the implications of faith are of a piece.

But how in the world can Paul write to faithful friends that God has graciously given to them the experience of suffering? This comes across as strange to ears of Westerners, who do all they can to avoid suffering, and when it does come, ask, "Why, O Lord?" Is the apostle glorifying suffering by labeling it a gracious gift to the Philippians?

First, we need to ask what Paul intends by suffering. With the possible exception of Rom 8:18–39, nowhere in Paul's letters do we find the word "suffering" denoting such tragedies as the horrors of provoked or unprovoked disasters, the demonic ravages of cancer, the terrors of earthquakes and tornadoes, or the sanctioned or unsanctioned violence of discrimination and war. Instead Paul lists a variety of physical trials and tribulations, mental stresses, and violent rejections, all incurred in the service of the gospel. The sufferings are not "bad things" that happen, but are the result of deliberate, voluntary discipleship. They are sufferings that could have been avoided, had one chosen to live a different way and not have followed Christ (cf. Gal 6:12).

But critical to Paul's understanding of this suffering incurred in the cause of the gospel is the notion that it is a bond that ties the believer to the crucified Christ. When writing of his own experience, the apostle occasionally lists his so-called hardship catalogues (see 1 Cor 4:9–13; 2 Cor 4:7–12; 11:23–29), which do not function as badges to confirm his valor in battle, but rather unite him with the crucified Jesus. "Constantly carrying in the body the dying of Jesus, so that the life of Jesus may also be made visible in our bodies" (2 Cor 4:10). Later in Philippians, he expresses his desire to "know Christ and the power of his resurrection and the sharing of his sufferings by becoming like him in his death" (3:10). Identification with the crucified and risen Jesus entails participation in his suffering.

[1:30] This gift of believing and suffering puts the readers in the same predicament as the apostle. Their sharing in the gospel from the first day until

Concern for the Recipients 47

now (1:5) thrusts them into the same "struggle" that Paul had undertaken in Philippi and that apparently has continued. Exactly what that "struggle" entails, Paul does not say (since the Philippians obviously knew), but the depiction in Acts of the conflict between Paul and exploiters of the slave girl, which landed him in prison, certainly fits the context (Acts 16:19–24; 1 Thess 2:2–4). The charge against Paul was anti-Roman conduct. If the parallel between the two passages is to be taken seriously, then most likely the Philippians are under threat from the imperial authorities, too. In this Roman colony, professing faith in Christ and living out that faith would leave one vulnerable to all manner of charges of anti-Roman conduct.

2:1–11 To Manifest Unity and Humility after the Manner of the Christ Event

[2:1–2] Paul continues to articulate his hopes for his readers by exhorting them a second time to maintain communal steadfastness and assuredness in the face of opposition. "Make my joy complete," he urges, and the dominant imperative makes clear that to accomplish Paul's behest, the Philippians must demonstrate intentional unity (2:2). The paragraph is highly structured, both before and after the imperative, giving the passage considerable force. Verse 1 lists four bases for unity: encouragement in Christ, comfort from love, participation in the Spirit, and compassion and mercy. The imperative is then immediately followed by a chiasm:

A Be of the same mind.
  B Have the same love
  B' Be of one accord.
A' Be of one mind.

[2:3–4] Verses 3–4 continue the exhortations in an alternating pattern of contrasts: *not* from selfish ambition or conceit *but (alla)* in humility, looking *not* to one's own interests only *but (alla)* also to the interests of others.

> 2:1 Therefore, since[a] there is encouragement in Christ, since there is comfort afforded by love, since there is sharing in the Spirit, since there is compassion and mercy, 2 make my joy complete by[b] having the same mind, by having the same love, by being of one accord, by having one mind. 3 Do nothing from selfishness or conceit, but in humility regard others as better than yourselves. 4 Each of you should look not to your own interests, but also[c] to the interests of others.

> a. The Greek reads *ei* and is normally rendered "if" (see NRSV and NIV); however, with the "therefore" there is no contingent or conditional quality to the sentence. Thus, I have used "since" in place of "if."

b. Because the four elements accompanying the chiasm (see above) are parallel, I have treated them as participles of means, stating how Paul's joy will be fulfilled. As a matter of fact, only two are participles. The first is a *hina* clause, indicating the nature of Paul's joy; the third is an adjective (*sympsychoi*), which might be translated with the adverb "wholeheartedly" or more colloquially rendered as "soul mates."

c. The *kai* ("also") is omitted in a few manuscripts of the Western family and in the NSRV. The reason seems to be that the editors assume that scribes introduced the *kai* to make the statement less radical. The Nestle-Aland (twenty-seventh edition) indicates the uncertainty by placing the *kai* in brackets. The strong manuscript evidence for its inclusion has led to my translation. Paul is certainly not advocating self-neglect, but rather is pointing to the priority of putting others ahead of ourselves.

The theme of unity, which the apostle has highlighted as a necessity in the face of opposition (1:27–30), is continued in 2:1–4, but with more of a theological foundation. Four bases are given for the unity Paul calls for among the Philippians. They are not discrete or distinct reasons, but in fact grow out of the readers' life in Christ. The first two terms—"encouragement" (*paraklēsis*) and "comfort" (*paramythion*)—are hardly distinguishable, particularly if "love" is understood to be Christ's love for the church and not primarily the believers' love for one another or their love for Christ. Actually, in calling them to live together in harmony Paul is appealing to the highest motive: the love that the Lord of the church has for his people, a love that enables them to live worthily.

The third expression ("sharing in the Spirit") has provoked considerable debate, as to whether "Spirit" is a subjective or an objective genitive. Is it a sharing given by the Spirit, or is it a participation in the Spirit? Schweizer is no doubt correct in contending that the two interpretations amount to the same thing.[9] The *koinōnia* is a gift of the Spirit, which is the divine indwelling in the church. Such common sharing should bring to an end any divisions and rivalry within the body of Christ.

The fourth God-given element that serves as the basis for unity comprises the two terms "compassion" (*splanchna*) and "mercy" (*oiktirmoi*). While the former (literally, "bowels"; cf. 1:8) expresses the passion one has for another, the second term, "mercies," is used elsewhere in Paul for the gracious attitude of God toward sinful humanity (Rom 12:1; 2 Cor 1:3). As believers recognize more and more their dependence on divine grace, they are enabled to express the unity and steadfastness needed in the church.

The imperative "make my joy complete" is an appeal to the implied readers as well as a reminder to modern readers of the critical theme of "joy" and "rejoicing" that permeates the entire letter. Paul rejoices in his prayers at the remembrance of these Philippians and their sharing in the work of the gospel with him (1:3–7). He even rejoices in his jail cell at the proclamation of the

---

9. Eduard Schweizer, "πνεῦμα," *TDNT*, 6:434.

Concern for the Recipients

ambitious preachers, who are out to make life harder for the apostle (1:15–18). He invites his readers now to live in unity, which in turn will "complete" or "fulfill" his joy. Just as God will "fulfill" every need of theirs (4:19), so Paul appeals to them to "fulfill" his joy.

The chiasm that follows the imperative elaborates the ways in which the unity of the church is to be expressed. The beginning and the ending of the chiasm interestingly call for a common "mind." Paul is not demanding a single theology, as if all church members are to think alike regarding matters of faith and life. He is rather asking for a commonality in their practical reasoning, which would entail a combination of their intellectual and affective lives, leading them to act in a certain way. It is a critical characteristic of their life together, as will be evident in 2:5. Furthermore, they are to exhibit the same love with which Christ loves them, which means being harmonious or living as "soul mates" (*sympsychoi*).

Whereas the earlier section (1:27–30) stresses the need for courage in the face of external opposition, with a particular concern for the public witness of the church, 2:1–4 is directed more toward relationships within the community. For example, the exhortations in 2:3–4 move beyond unity to speak of humility. "Do nothing from selfishness or conceit, but in humility regard others as better than yourselves" (2:3).

Humility is a crucial matter in Philippians; the word occurs in the letter in various forms four times (2:3, 8; 3:21; 4:1; *tapeinos* or *tapeinophrosynē*). In the Greco-Roman culture the term is primarily used in a disparaging way. Humility expresses the low estate of a person living in poor and petty circumstances, often a slave. It signifies that which is lowly, weak, mean, and trivial. The problem is that such a person acquires a servile disposition and becomes an obsequious flatterer to be pitied by people of position.[10]

In contrast, Jewish and Christian literature both present a positive approach toward humility, in relation to God and to other people. In the first place, humility describes the proper human response to God, to whom service and obedience are owed. Often in the Old Testament, it is associated with fasting, expressing abasement before God (e.g., Lev 16:29, 31; Isa 58:3, 5). The people of Qumran even referred to themselves as "the poor," "the humble," "the lowly," and "the afflicted" to express their dependence on divine mercy (e.g., 1QH 5:13–22; 1QS 5:3–4). Furthermore, Jesus spoke of himself as "gentle and humble in heart" (Matt 11:29).

As for 2:3–4, the opposite of humility means living out of *eritheia*, a contentiousness characteristic of those who preach the gospel from untoward motives and want to make life hard for the apostle (1:17), and *kenodoxia*, empty conceit born of an exaggerated sense of self.

---

10. See the discussion in Walter Grundmann, "ταπεινός," *TDNT*, 8:1–60.

Humility in Philippians, however, takes on a christological orientation, in light of the following Christ hymn (2:6–11). It becomes a quality advocated for members of the Christian community because of the Christ who "humbled himself and became obedient unto the point of death" (2:8). In practical terms, it involves moving beyond a preoccupation with one's own affairs to a concern for the interests of others. It means valuing their needs and achievements above one's own. Rather than being a mark of weakness, humility in the light of Christ becomes a mark of strength. Barth poignantly writes:

> The reason why we are to see the other's point of view, to let ourselves be enticed out of our own hut and over into his, is not that that were supposedly a holy place, but it is only when men [and women] thus come together, when they take a joint view of things, when they bow jointly before him who is greater than both my neighbor and myself—it is only then that the really holy, true, and helpful One comes into my field of vision at all. It is not until I see the other's point of view that I myself really see. . . . Always my neighbor is the barrier, but also the door. There is no road that passes by him.[11]

2:5–11 The "Christ Hymn"

Philippians 2:5–11 has often confused New Testament scholars and provoked debate about a number of issues. While there is general agreement that it represents a hymn of some sort, there is disagreement over whether Paul wrote the hymn or whether it is a hymn he adopted from the early church. What lies behind the hymn? Is it a reflection of texts from Isaiah or from Genesis or from neither? Does the hymn relate the preexistence of Jesus, or does it parallel the story of Adam and the account of his disobedience in the garden of Eden? How does the hymn function in the letter of Philippians? Is it an ethical exhortation to live a humble life as Jesus did, or does the hymn relate the story of salvation, which calls the church into being? These are a few of the issues that have baffled scholars and created considerable hand-wringing.

We begin with a translation of the text.

2:5 Let your bearing toward one another arise out of your life in Christ Jesus,[a]
    6 who, though being in the form of God,
        did not consider equality with God
        as something to be exploited,
    7 but emptied himself,
        taking the form of a slave,
becoming in the likeness of humans.[b]
And being found in the human state,

---

11. Barth et al., *Philippians*, 59.

8   he humbled himself,
      becoming obedient unto death.
      even death on a cross.
9   Wherefore God also raised him to the highest place
      and graciously gave him the name
      that is above every name,
10 that at the name of Jesus
      every knee should bow
      in heaven, on earth, and under the earth
11 and every tongue confess[c]
      that Jesus Christ is Lord,
      to the glory of God the Father.

a. I have followed the NEB translation of 2:5, which more literally might be rendered, "Let the same mind be in you that you have in Christ Jesus" (NRSV margin). My clear preference is for "have" as the verb to be used in the ellipsis rather than "was" (as in NRSV and NIV), but see the discussion below. The *en Christō Iēsou* is to be understood in its full soteriological sense regularly used by the apostle (Phil 1:1, 26; 3:3, 14; 4:7, 19). "Christology is viewed here within the framework of soteriology."[12] *Phroneite* connotes more than simply "to think," but takes on an affective dimension as well as an intellectual one. Note the double appearance of the word in 2:2.

b. There is no real reason to select the singular, read by P[46] and a few other early witnesses. As Metzger explains, "It is more likely that the singular number is merely a non-doctrinal accommodation to the singular δούλου and the following ἄνθρωπος."[13]

c. The verb can be taken as a future passive indicative (*exomologesetai*) or as an aorist subjunctive (*exomologēsetai*). The manuscript evidence is about evenly divided. The aorist subjunctive parallels *kampsē* ("bow") in 2:10. The change to the aorist subjunctive could have been intended to bring the two verbs in line with each other, or a scribe could have been influenced by Isa 45:23, where both verbs—*kampsei* and *exomologēsetai*—are in the future indicative. In either case, the meaning is not changed.

[2:5] How is 2:5 to be translated? Martin prefers "the best neutral rendering": the RSV ("Have this mind among yourselves which you have in Christ Jesus.")[14] The translation actually depends on the Christology of the passage. If one takes the hymn as only a model of humility presented as an ideal to be imitated, for readers to follow, then one covers the ellipsis with some form of the verb "to be" (so KJV and NIV). If, on the other hand, one is inclined to think that the readers are being called to live a new life out of the story of salvation depicted

---

12. Ernst Käsemann, "A Critical Analysis of Philippians 2:5–11," *JTC* 5 (1968): 65.
13. Bruce M. Metzger, *A Textual Commentary on the Greek New Testament* (2d ed.; Stuttgart: United Bible Societies, 1994), 546.
14. Ralph P. Martin, *A Hymn of Christ: Philippians 2:5–11 in Recent Interpretation and in the Setting of Early Christian Worship* (Downers Grove, Ill.: InterVarsity, 1997), xlviii.

in the hymn, then some other verb (such as "have") more fittingly suits the context. The NEB seems direct in pointing the readers to the "in Christ Jesus" as a typically Pauline soteriological formula. The issue is not a concern regarding the relationship of Father to Son in the Godhead, but with the fact that readers belong to his lordship and that now they can obey the one to whom praise is offered. Christology is set forth in the framework of soteriology.

The critical imperative in 2:5 is *phroneite*, which connotes not simply intellectual activity but practical thought or reasoning, a focus on the heart as well as the brain, on action as well as thinking. What the believers in Philippi are enjoined to do is to live out the story of salvation in Christ and to let their lives be shaped by such a story. As Wayne Meeks comments, "The letter's most comprehensive purpose is the shaping of a Christian *phronēsis*, a practical moral reasoning that is conformed to his [Christ's] death in hope of his resurrection."[15]

[2:6–8] At 2:6 the hymn[16] begins. First, a word about its literary character, those features of the text that are significant. One is the definition and determination of the *form* of the text. Rather universally, scholars recognize the "who" (*hos*, 2:6) as the beginning of a poetic structure. The remainder of the passage reflects a stately rhythmic pattern, marked by striking parallelisms, sometimes complementary, sometimes contrasting. We do not know enough about the worship in the early church to label 2:6–11 a "hymn," except in a general sense. It might have functioned as a creedal statement or as a liturgical formula, perhaps recited in worship.

Can the passage be divided into strophes with the appropriate stresses? The scholarly answer is yes, but then the options are numerous. It has been divided into six strophes of three lines each;[17] into three strophes of four lines each;[18] into six strophes of two lines each;[19] and into a chiastic pattern of four strophes, the first and last of six lines, the second and third of four lines each.[20] Several scholars suggest that Paul has edited a traditional hymn by adding the following phrases: "even death on a cross" (2:8); "in heaven and on earth" (2:10); and "to the glory of God the Father" (2:11).

Did Paul himself compose this hymn, or is it to be treated as pre-Pauline? Paul is certainly capable of writing high prose, such as Rom 8:31–39 or 1 Cor 13. But because of key expressions in the hymn that appear here and nowhere else in Paul

---

15. Meeks, "Man from Heaven in Philippians," 333.
16. I use the traditional designation "hymn," though this terminology is not recognized by all scholars as descriptive of this passage.
17. Ernst Lohmeyer, *Kyrios Jesus: Eine Untersuchung zur Phil. 2, 5–11* (2d ed.; SHAW 4; Heidelberg: C. Winter, 1961), 4–13.
18. Joachim Jeremias, "Zu Philipper 2,7: ἑαυτὸν ἐκένωσεν," in *Abba: Studien zur neutestamentlichen Theologie und Zeitgeschichte* (Göttingen: Vandenhoeck & Ruprecht, 1966), 38–39.
19. Martin, *Hymn of Christ*, 36–38.
20. Morna D. Hooker, *From Adam to Christ* (London: SCM Press, 1990), 88–100.

Concern for the Recipients

(such as *morphē*) or nowhere else even in the New Testament (such as *harpagmos, hyperypsoō, katachthonios*), and because it concludes with an exaltation of Jesus, with no mention of the typically Pauline pattern of the resurrection and return of Jesus, I am inclined to think it pre-Pauline.[21] It is somewhat surprising, however, that so many recent commentators treat the hymn as Pauline.[22]

The second literary feature of the passage to note is its *narrative* quality. It relates the story of Christ, from his being in the form of God and deciding that equality with God was not something to be exploited, through his self-emptying by taking the form of a slave and being born in human likeness, to his obedience unto death. Jesus' career is continued in 2:9–11, but now with God as the primary subject, exalting Christ and giving him the supreme name at whose articulation all the hosts of heaven and earth, both cosmic and human, are to bow in obeisance. He is Lord, to the glory of God. The narrative of Christ's career has then two major movements: humiliation (2:6–8) and exaltation (2:9–11).

The way in which the first movement of humiliation is depicted sounds a great deal like the story of the Suffering Servant (Isa 52:13–53:12) or the story of Adam (Gen 1:26–27; 3:5). Could either be the model for the Christ of the hymn?

The problem with seeing the Suffering Servant as the background and model for 2:6–11 is the fact that the Septuagint does not use the word *doulos* (2:7) for "servant" but instead uses the word *pais*. Moreover, in Isa 52:13 where the expression "my servant" appears, it functions as a title of honor and not of degradation as in Phil 2:7. The figure in Isaiah dies a shameful death, to be sure, yet there is no indication that he does this as a result of his status as God's servant. Thus, it is virtually impossible in the story of humiliation to discover in the hymn a reference to the Suffering Servant.

But could Adam somehow function as the model for 2:6–11? After all, he was created in the "image of God" and responded to the serpent's appeal by snatching at the opportunity to enhance his own status, to "be like God" (though in the Genesis story Eve is the one who is tempted with the words "for when you eat of it, your eyes will be opened and you will be like God" [Gen 3:5]). Adam's decision resulted in his losing what he had and becoming a slave to corruption and death (cf. Wis 2:23–24). Christ, on the other hand, is the last Adam (Rom 5:12–21; 1 Cor 15:21–22, 44–49), who did not choose as the first Adam had chosen, but instead freely accepted the consequences of the first Adam's choice. He made himself powerless, in response to which God exalted him.

The Christ of Phil 2:6–11 therefore is the man who undid Adam's wrong: confronted with the same choice, he rejected Adam's sin, but nevertheless

---

21. See A. M. Hunter, *Paul and His Predecessors* (Philadelphia: Westminster, 1961), 39–44; Martin, *Hymn of Christ*, lv–lxx; Richard N. Longenecker, *New Wine into Fresh Wineskins: Contextualizing the Early Christian Confessions* (Peabody, Mass.: Hendrickson, 1999), 49–50.

22. See Caird, *Letters from Prison*, 98–104; Bockmuehl, *Philippians*, 117–20; Fee, *Philippians*, 45–46, among others.

freely followed Adam's course as fallen man to the bitter end of death—wherefore God bestowed on him the status that Adam lost, but the status which Adam was intended to come to: God's final prototype, the last Adam.[23]

The critical issue in this reading of the hymn is the rendering of 2:6. How can it be said that Adam was "in the form of God"?[24] Dunn contends that "form" (*morphē*), "image" (*eikōn*), and "glory" (*doxa*) are virtually interchangeable in the Septuagint, and that in 2:6 Adam is in the "form of God" in the sense of Gen 1:27 ("in the image of God he created them"). Furthermore, the word *harpagmos* (NRSV: "something to be exploited") is to be understood, according to Dunn, with reference to something not yet possessed, something to be grasped de novo, a robbery. Thus, Adam and the earthly Jesus are both in the image of God. Adam heeds the serpent's invitation and grasps after God but ends up a fallen creature—that is, in human likeness and in the form of a slave. Christ, on the other hand, resists the temptation to grasp after equality with God and humbly takes on the plight of fallen humanity.

The difficulty with Dunn's reading of the hymn is that it does not hold up linguistically. "Form" (*morphē*) and "image" (*eikōn*) turn out not to be synonyms in the LXX. In fact, whenever in the LXX the Bible speaks about humanity as the image of God, *eikōn* is used and never *morphē*.[25] Moreover, while the Latin fathers tended to render *harpagmos* as "plundering, usurpation, or robbery," most other scholars take it as denoting "something greedily clung to" or "something to be exploited" (NRSV).[26] Equality with God is something that Christ already possessed but chose not to use for his own advantage.

Another treatment of the hymn also follows the Adam parallels, but limits the connection to a single point. The contrast is drawn between Adam, who grasped at equality with God, a dignity to which he had no right, and Christ, who did not take advantage of a status to which he had every right, but humbled himself unto death on a cross. This treatment of the hymn allows for a traditional reading of the preexistence of Christ and enables the hymn to function more credibly in the context of exhortation set in 2:1–5.[27] Yet, as we shall see, Adam Christology does not fit with the second movement of the hymn (2:9–11).

We are thus left with the traditional reading of the hymn, which entails Jesus' preexistence, meaning that he has some sort of extra-mortal life prior to being born as a human. What that extra-mortal existence involved, we are not told,

---

23. James D. G. Dunn, *Christology in the Making: A New Testament Inquiry into the Origins of the Doctrine of the Incarnation* (Philadelphia: Westminster, 1980), 119.

24. Ibid., 115.

25. Dave Steenburg, "The Case against the Synonymity of Morphe and Eikon," *JSNT* 34 (1988): 77–86.

26. R. W. Hoover, "The *Harpagmos* Enigma: A Philosophical Solution," *HTR* 64 (1971): 95–119.

27. See Caird, *Letters from Prison*, 118–24, and Wright, ed., *Climax*, 56–98.

Concern for the Recipients

nor is such preexistence crucial to our understanding of the hymn. One can compare the verse from 2 Corinthians, where in soliciting the offering for the Jerusalem church, Paul writes, "You know the generous act of our Lord Jesus Christ, that though he was rich, yet for your sakes he became poor, so that by his poverty you might become rich" (2 Cor 8:9). In Phil 2:6 Jesus was "in the form of God," which is the same as "being equal to God," and yet he did not consider "equality with God" a thing to be exploited or taken advantage of.

The phrase *isa theō* ("equal to God") is probably to be taken as a social category rather than one of nature or essence. Though the creeds of the later church insisted that Jesus was "of one essence with the Father" in order to affirm that humans had been confronted in Jesus with no one less than God himself, it would be a mistake to read the councils of Nicaea and Chalcedon back into Philippians. The issue does not have to do with nature or essence, but with status. So, Jesus' emptying of himself is explained in terms of his becoming incarnate, his taking the "form of a slave," meaning his subjection to the demonic forces that deprive humans of their freedom. What he leaves behind is his status, not his deity. In fact, one could say he shows himself to be "equal to God" precisely in his obedience that led him to the shameful death on a cross, the ultimate point of faithfulness to the One with whom he shared equality.

Perhaps the most difficult question regarding the hymn is how it functions in the letter. The issue becomes particularly sharp when we recognize that the hymn does not address a christological problem, as does (for instance) the hymn in Colossians (1:15–20). The immediate context in Philippians is hortatory (1:27–2:18, and especially 2:1–5). Philippians 2:5 is controlled by an imperative (*phroneite*, "set your mind on"). The history of research has posed a number of suggestions about the function of the hymn. The more important proposals warrant our careful attention.

An initial suggestion interprets the hymn (2:6–11) as an ethical model to be followed. In the story of the Christ we have the supreme example of one who did nothing from selfish ambition or conceit, but in humility regarded others as better than himself, one who looked not to his own interests but to the interests of others (2:1–4). Philippians 2:5 then could be translated, "Let the same mind be in you that was in Christ" (NRSV), with the verb "to be" covering the ellipsis. Jesus' act of self-emptying and becoming obedient unto death on a cross serves as an ideal that believers at Philippi are to imitate. As Lohmeyer comments, Jesus' obedience unto death is therefore "the divine proof of an exemplary life."[28] The problem with this proposal is its almost naïve idealism, as well as its failure to account for the second half of the hymn (2:9–11). Are those who follow Jesus to be exalted as he was and given a name that is above all names?

---

28. Lohmeyer, *Kyrios Jesus*, 42.

A more recent proposal, made by Stephen Fowl,[29] acknowledges the danger of ethical idealism, but at the same time takes the hortatory context seriously. Fowl contends that the hymn does not function as a static model but as an "exemplar," a term he borrows from T. S. Kuhn. Instead of being an abstract, lawlike generalization, an "exemplar" is a concrete formulation, normative for a community (in Kuhn's case, a community of scientists), which can be extended by analogy to offer solutions to other particular problems. The story of Christ in 2:6–11 is a concrete description of the Lord in whom the Philippians believe. But in the context (1:27–2:18), appropriate analogies are drawn from it that are applicable to their situation. Christ's actions become the warrant as well as the paradigm for the actions that Paul urges on his readers. (Fowl has apparently changed his mind regarding the hymn, since in his recent commentary on Philippians he suggests that scholars drop the claim that 2:6–11 is a quotation of preexisting material, and he does not mention Kuhn's name at all.)[30]

As for the second half of the hymn, Fowl follows Hurtado in saying that these verses state the divine vindication and approval of the actions taken in 2:6–11. They do not represent an epilogue to 2:6–8, but serve "to evaluate Jesus' obedience in the highest terms."[31] Or as Bultmann has put it, Jesus promises a "reward" to those who are obedient without thought of a reward.[32]

Over against the proposals that have highlighted an *imitatio Christi* pattern, Käsemann some time ago contended that from the beginning the hymn declared an event that had happened, a drama that had taken place. Words like "he humbled himself" and "he emptied himself" are not, however, events from the life of the historical Jesus that believers are to emulate. They rather describe the saving acts of a Redeemer figure in a gnostic mythological framework, which has been Christianized to suit the context. The obedience that the Redeemer demonstrates is not primarily for human imitation, but to bring to light the miracle of the saving story. "He reveals obedience but does not demonstrate it as something to be imitated. To put it succinctly, he is *Urbild*, not *Vorbild*; archetype, not model."[33] Furthermore, the expression "in Jesus Christ" at the end of v. 5 is to be taken in terms of its full soteriological usage in Paul, rather than in a limited christological sense.

---

29. Stephen E. Fowl, *The Story of Christ in the Ethics of Paul: An Analysis of the Function of the Hymnic Material in the Pauline Corpus* (JSNTSup 36; Sheffield: JSOT, 1990), 77–101.

30. Stephen E. Fowl, *Philippians* (THNTC; Grand Rapids: Eerdmans, 2005), 112.

31. Larry W. Hurtado, "Jesus' Lordly Example in Phil. 2:5–11," in *From Jesus to Paul: Studies in Honour of Francis Wright Beare* (ed. Peter Richardson and John Coolidge Hurd; Waterloo, Ontario, Canada: Wilfrid Laurier University Press, 1984), 125.

32. Rudolf Bultmann, *Theology of the New Testament* (trans. Kendrick Grobel; 2 vols.; New York: Scribner, 1951), 1:79.

33. Käsemann, "Philippians 2:5–11," 72.

Emptying himself and being found in the likeness of humans (Jesus' *kenōsis*) entails a particular mission for Jesus: "taking the form of a slave" (2:7). One recalls the slavery to the elemental spirits mentioned in Gal 4:8–9; Rom 8:15. The one who was far superior to all these superhuman spirits became just as subject to them as anyone else.[34] And yet his obedience "even to the cross" makes this event a saving one and not merely an ideal to be copied by his followers (cf. 1 Cor 1:18). As Käsemann comments, "The second stanza shows that what matters is not just the correct ethical attitude but victory over the world, which is to say, the elimination of the anti-divine forces standing in the way of eschatological fulfillment."[35]

In the concluding section of his essay, Käsemann begins to face the question of the significance of the story represented in the hymn for the Philippian readers. Christ became obedient and is now exalted over the world in his present status as "Lord," having subdued all the cosmic forces that trouble and distress humans. While the hymn employs the framework of a Hellenistic myth, it differs in one critical point—its eschatological motif. "It speaks of nothing less than the end of the old age when [humanity] is under the dominion of evil forces and the beginning of the New Aeon, wherein all the hostile powers are defeated."[36] The church is caught up into the eschatological event and is a witness on earth to the enthronement of the one who was obedient, even to death on a cross.

Käsemann's interpretation of the passage is to be preferred over the others for at least two reasons. One is the clear avoidance of an ethical idealism, a pit into which many moralistic interpreters fall. The fact that scholarship today questions a pre-Christian gnostic myth does not invalidate the fact that the passage relates the saga of divine salvation. "The hymn does not communicate who Jesus was christologically as much as what he did soteriologically. The dramatic impact of this event makes it all the more difficult to imagine imitation as a goal, since followers could not realistically hope to repeat the redemptive act and exaltation of Christ."[37] The story includes Jesus' obedience unto death, but as the prelude to his ultimate reward. He is enthroned by divine appointment and is given the very name of YHWH himself.

Those to whom the parenesis is addressed are not exhorted to be humble simply because they have in Christ a model of humility. Paul directs his exhortation to persons who live in a cosmos that is being changed by God's exaltation of Christ. Reading the whole hymn as fundamental to the parenesis, we can see

---

34. Osiek, *Philippians*, 62.
35. Käsemann, "Philippians 2:5–11," 49.
36. Martin, *Hymn of Christ*, 92.
37. Joseph A. Marchal, "Expecting a Hymn, Encountering an Argument: Introducing the Rhetoric of Philippians and Pauline Interpretation," *Int* 61 (2007): 247.

that Paul's addressees are encouraged to live in a world the hostile powers of which are in the process of being subjected to the kenotic Christ.[38]

[2:9–11] Second, the exaltation theme of the hymn makes much better sense in Käsemann's rendering than in any other. Jesus is not here exalted to the human dominion given at creation (Gen 1:28), "but to the uniquely divine sovereignty which is acknowledged by all creation when God's sole deity as the one and only God is universally confessed."[39] This may be the earliest place in the New Testament where Jesus is worshiped as God (see also 1 Cor 8:6). No doubt lurking behind 2:9–11 is Isa 45:21–23, where the standard monotheistic formula is repeated three times ("There is no one besides me," 45:21), and the allusion in Philippians is clearly to Isa 45:23 ("To me every knee shall bow, every tongue shall swear"). Since the Isaiah reference demands that the name that is above every name must be YHWH, so in Phil 2:10–11 the name every tongue confesses is not Jesus, but "Lord" (YHWH), the name of status and power (see Phil 1:2, 14; 2:19, 29; 3:8, 20; 4:1, 2, 4, 5, 10, 23).[40] "The eschatological monotheistic expectation of Deutero-Isaiah and Second Temple Judaism is fulfilled through the revelation of Jesus' inclusion in the unique divine identity. Eschatological monotheism proves to be christological monotheism."[41]

As Bauckham points out,[42] this excludes Dunn's reading of the passage in terms of Adam Christology, as well as Wright's attempt to combine an Adam Christology with a recognition of the monotheistic significance of the allusion to Isa 45:23. Adam does not figure in Isa 45 at all.

At the same time the high Christology expressed in the hymn is confessed "to the glory of God the Father" (2:11). The descending/ascending Lord acts at the behest and to the honor of God, who as the divine actor in the second movement of the hymn makes it all possible. Jesus becomes the object of worship because God reveals God's self through the One obedient to the cross.

The word "confess" (*exomologēsētai*) likely does not imply praise with thanksgiving, as Lightfoot contended,[43] but rather the more general "admit,

---

38. J. Louis Martyn, *De-apocalypticizing Paul: An Essay Focused on Paul and the Stoics by Troels Engberg-Pedersen*, JSNT 24, no. 86 (2001–2): 84.

39. Richard Bauckham, "The Worship of Jesus in Philippians 2:9–11," in *Where Christology Began: Essays on Philippians 2* (ed. Ralph P. Martin and Brian J. Dodd; Louisville, Ky.: Westminster John Knox, 1998), 134.

40. There is a difference between the Greek understanding of *kyrios* (Lord) and the Hebrew understanding of YHWH (Lord). *Kyrios* can be understood to be many things: among them, slave owner and master. YHWH is the name by which God is known in the Old Testament, and it is this name of Lord that will be transferred to Jesus at the time of his return. Further, the worship of the one God "was a recognition of God's unique identity, which itself had to be characterized in other terms" (Bauckham, "Worship," 137).

41. Ibid., 133.

42. Ibid., 139.

43. Lightfoot, *Philippians*, 115.

acknowledge openly."[44] This allows the angelic powers to whom Jesus has been the slave to admit openly and irrevocably that God has established him as the rightful Lord of the universe. They are not making a confession of faith in the contemporary sense of that expression; they are merely alien powers that are capitulating to the obvious. "It is their response to the divine epiphany which declares the sovereignty of the lordly Christ; and it is a response that they dutifully, if unwillingly, make."[45]

How then does this hymn fit into the context of 2:1–18, with its emphasis on unity, humility, and the working out of our "salvation"? Rather than presenting an ethical model to be followed, an ideal to be imitated, the hymn first announces the defeat of the forces that enslave humans and then declares the lordship of Christ. Having heard and responded to such a One who gave himself in obedience, even to the cross, the community "in Christ" then has the freedom to be of the "same mind," to submit to one another, to value others more highly than oneself.

The imperative is significant in Phil 2:5. As the world is being changed and the hostile powers are being confronted by the preaching of the kenotic Christ, unity, humility, and steadfastness can become a reality for the church. And yet the opposition posed by the civil authorities is heightened by the confession of Jesus as Lord. Just as Paul and Silas were arrested for "acting contrary to the decrees of the emperor, saying that there is another king named Jesus" (Acts 17:7), so the Philippians are placed in a more vulnerable position by the reciting of this hymn. The saga of salvation is not an escape, but an empowerment for the church. It is a privileged obligation that the church engage in mission and remain unified and steadfast in the face of opposition.

This passage is designated as the epistolary reading for Palm/Passion Sunday for all three years in the Common Lectionary. It is often bypassed as the choice for a sermon text because of the traditional observance on this Sunday of Jesus' triumphal entry into Jerusalem, and yet its hymnic character lends it for use in the Palm Sunday parade. It sings of the story of Christ's humiliation, in not clinging to the divine prerogative but taking the form of a slave, and of God's response in exalting him to a place of prominence above all principalities and powers. What more majestic hymn has the church to sing than this one?

2:12–18 Concern for the Recipients

The paragraphs that immediately follow the hymn (2:12–13, 14–18) are linked to it by a consequential particle ("therefore"), and thus they continue the hortatory section begun at 1:27. The community that has been exhorted to unity

---

44. Bauer and Danker, eds., BDAG, 351.
45. Martin, *Hymn of Christ*, 264.

and harmony and to have courage in the face of opposition is told to work out its own "salvation" and to live without complaint and argument.

2:12 Therefore, my beloved ones, just as you have always been obedient, not only when[a] I have been with you, but now much more in my absence, continue to work out[b] your salvation with fear and trembling. **13** For God is the one who is at work among you both to will and to accomplish his good pleasure. **14** Continue to do all things without murmuring and complaining, **15** that you may be blameless and innocent, children of God without blemish in the midst of a crooked and distorted generation, in which you shine as luminaries in the world, **16** holding forth[c] the word of life, that you may be for me a reason for boasting in the day of Christ, because I did not run in vain nor have I labored in vain. **17** But even if I am poured out as a libation on the sacrifice and service of your faith, I am glad and rejoice with you all. In the same way, you also rejoice and celebrate together with me.

a. The *hos* has strong manuscript evidence and is only omitted by scribes who apparently thought it superfluous.

b. The imperative "work out" in 2:12 is in the present tense and suggests ongoing action. So "continue to work out." Likewise in 2:14: "Continue to do all things. . . ."

c. The participle *epechontes* can be translated "holding on to" (so NRSV "holding fast to"). Here, however, the emphasis seems to be on the mission of the Philippian Christians, who are exhorted to live blamelessly as lights in the midst of a darkened world. They do this by "holding forth" the word of life. The participle is often used of "holding forth a cup to someone's lips" or of "the offering a breast to a baby." See Homer, *Il.* 9.489; Homer, *Il.* 22.83.[46] Here the Philippians are exhorted to "hold forth the word of life." This is how they shine as luminaries in the midst of a dark and twisted world.

[2:12–13] Several features demand special comment in this paragraph that follows the hymn. First, what does Paul mean by "work out your own salvation"? Is he implying that the individual must work at his or her own eschatological, personal salvation? But this seems to violate the concern of the letter as well as the immediate context, which is clearly plural. The letter is addressed to the whole community, which is to work at its wholeness, integrity, and unity, together, as one body, even under duress. What is significant is that the church's task is called "salvation," a loaded theological term.

---

46. For further examples, see James P. Ware, "'Holding Forth the Word of Life': Paul and the Mission of the Church in the Letter to the Philippians in the Context of Second Temple Judaism" (UMI Dissertation Services, 1996), 291–92.

Concern for the Recipients

A second feature comes in the phrase "with fear and trembling" (2:12). In the three other occasions where these words occur in the Pauline corpus, they describe the healthy respect one has or should have for a human group with whom one is working (1 Cor 2:3; 2 Cor 7:15; Eph 6:5), a respect also evident in the Old Testament pairing of similar words (cf. Gen 9:2; Exod 15:16; Deut 2:25; 11:25). Barth calls this "startled humility, the consciousness of having nothing to assert in one's favor and against the others."[47] Since in 2:13 God is the ultimate actor in the working out of salvation, one cannot rule out the elements of honor, awe, and reverence in the presence of God. Awe before God goes together with humility before one's sisters and brothers in Christ.

A third feature in this paragraph is the paradox between the imperative "work out your own salvation" and the assurance that "God is at work in you" (v. 13). On the one hand, the community is to struggle for unity and integrity in its life in the world, even when it faces opposition. The second sentence does not lessen the demands of the first command. On the other hand, 2:13 unequivocally affirms the operative element of divine grace. God is the empowering presence who enables the community to do God's will. As Paul put it in the prayer of thanksgiving (1:6), "the one who began in you a good work will bring it to completion at the day of Christ." As they stand side by side and strive for the unity of the faith, the Philippians can be assured that "the real Accomplisher of all real salvation" is at work among them.[48]

"Works" are certainly not denigrated in Philippians. Grace is not set over against the doing of good works, as seems to be the case in Eph 2:8–10. Rather, good deeds are the result of God's activity in the Christian community, God's pushing and shoving us to accomplish what he has intended us to be and to do.

[2:14–15] The church is described here in terms of its mission to the immediate world around it. Paul becomes very practical in stating his case. The Philippians are to live without grumbling and disputes so that they may be blameless and innocent. Paul uses this word "grumbling" in 1 Cor 10:10, when he cites as a warning to the Corinthians the occasion of Israel's complaining when they doubted that Moses could lead them to the promised land.[49] It denotes complaints made in behind-the-scene murmurings, whereas "disputes" entail "verbal exchanges when conflicting ideas are expressed."[50] Each occasion of this word in the Pauline corpus carries a negative connotation, such as the expression of "darkened minds" that have become futile in their "reasonings" (Rom 1:21).

---

47. Barth et al., *Philippians*, 72.
48. Ibid., 73.
49. Exod 16:1–12; 17:1–7.
50. Bauer and Danker, eds., BDAG, 233.

Is there any situation in Philippi that would warrant Paul's warning regarding "grumbling" and "disputes"? The disagreement between Euodia and Syntyche mentioned in 4:2 is not depicted in such strong language as is used in 2:14, and thus the apostle seems to be speaking to the community in general. The present imperative ("continue to do all things") suggests that they are not now guilty of "grumblings and disputes," but are being warned about the future. "Grumblings" and "disputes" can lead to serious splits within the church. Paul's intention is that the church end up being "without blame" and "children of God without blemish." He cites in 2:15 the accusing words of Moses in his farewell speech: "They have sinned; they are not his children; they are blemished; they are a crooked and perverse generation" (Deut 32:5, LXX). The Philippians text, however, affirms that if the readers will refrain from grumbling, they will be the children of God and without blemish. The final phrase from the Mosaic quotation ("a crooked and perverse generation") describes the world into which the readers are called to mission.

[2:16] In this context the church is to be a light in the midst of a dark world. The participle *epechontes* can be translated as "holding fast to" or "holding forth." A good case can be made for the latter rendering since the word's basic meaning has to do with extending or offering something to someone.[51] The Philippians are to hold forth "the word of life," an expression of the gospel, and as they do so, they shine as lights in a darkened and distorted world. One is reminded of Jesus' words in the Sermon on the Mount, "You are the light of the world" (Matt 5:14–15) and of Isa 42:6 and Isa 49:6 where Israel shines as a light to the Gentiles, drawing them to God. Furthermore, in Acts 13:47 Paul and Barnabas cite Isa 49:6 as a reason for their turning to the Gentiles.

As Ware contends,[52] nowhere else in Paul's letters are churches commanded to preach the gospel or to engage in missionary activity, except here, where the command is to "hold forth the word of life." In his letter to the Thessalonians, the apostle commends the Thessalonians for spreading the word but nowhere commands them to do so. This would imply that the Philippians' "partnership in the gospel" from the first day until the present (Phil 1:3–5) included much more than financial gifts; it had to do with their missionary activity in spreading the gospel. Ware argues, "Only to the church at Philippi, where the church's mission was in danger of being silenced, does Paul give an explicit mission command (2:16a)."[53] On the one hand, this may be Paul's only statement like unto a "great commission," but on the other hand, Paul's sense of responsibility to "win" both Jews and Gentiles to Christ is not limited to Philippians. In 1 Cor 9:19–23, Paul repeatedly uses the verb "win" (*kerdainō*), a "technical

---

51. See Ware, "Holding Forth," 291–92.
52. Ibid., 301.
53. Ibid., 303.

missionary term," implying the calling to faith those who have strayed.[54] Nevertheless, Ware is helpful in stressing the element of mission in Philippians.

The Philippians' engagement in mission then becomes Paul's "reason for boasting [*kauchēma*] in the day of Christ" (2:16) and proof that he has not run in vain or labored in vain. He is sure that his work will come under scrutiny on the day of judgment, and he feels equally assured that the churches of Macedonia will be his pride and joy in the eschatological judgment (cf. 1 Thess 2:19–20). Paul did not consider himself the primary missionary, but he did consider his converts "as the new mediatorial community for the salvation of the nations."[55] Though there is no immediate parallel to "word of life" elsewhere in Paul, he was convinced that through the gospel he had preached, the believers at Philippi would in turn preach that gospel to the world.

[2:17–18] Even if Paul is poured out as a libation on the sacrifice and service of the Philippians' faith, he still wants to rejoice and to have the Philippians join him in the celebration. The imagery here no doubt comes from the cultic language either of the Old Testament (Num 28:1–8; Exod 29:38–41) or of pagan sacrificial practice, where the priest completes the sacrifice by pouring out a libation of wine or oil over the offering. Whether Paul is thinking about his death as that libation, or whether he contemplates further service to the church (the present tense of the verb *spendomai* would suggest the latter), he is clearly mingling his acts of faith with the Philippians'. Such faithfulness is the occasion for rejoicing on his part as well as on the part of the Philippians. The mutuality of their joy is stressed both at the end of 2:17 and in 2:18. As Fowl comments, "Fidelity in the face of death or any other enemy is a cause for joy."[56]

We have in chapter 2, then, an example of Philippians as a community-building letter. Paul wants to nurture in his readers a vision of what it means to be a Christian congregation, stars shining in a dark sky, holding forth the word of life. They are to do all things without murmuring and disputing, not being preoccupied with their own affairs but in humility tending to the interests of others. Rather than being caught up in selfish ambition, they are to live humbly. This is possible for them because of the story of Christ, whose humiliation and exaltation have broken the power of the old age and have ushered in a new age in which he is Lord and in which the readers can manifest the unity and steadfastness needed to counter their enemies. God is the empowering presence to enable the community both to will and to accomplish his divine intention.

---

54. David Jacobus Bosch, *Transforming Mission: Paradigm Shifts in Theology of Mission* (ASMS 16; Maryknoll, N.Y.: Orbis, 1991), 525.

55. Ware, "Holding Forth," 326.

56. Fowl, *Philippians*, 129.

2:19–30 Travel Plans and Examples to Be Followed

Travelogue

The so-called travelogue section of Philippians contains a commendation of Timothy whom Paul hopes to send to the Philippians soon (2:19–23), a word about Paul's own hopes in visiting Philippi (2:24), and a supportive word about Epaphroditus, who is returning home and apparently serves as the courier for the letter (2:25–29). The statements made about Timothy and Epaphroditus are effusive and are likely intended to provide models for the Philippians to follow.

Paul's letters often contain his plans for visiting congregations in the future. Sometimes they function as a carrot or a stick to prod the congregation into action (Phlm 22; 2 Cor 13:10). On other occasions, they simply provide information about Paul and his projected itinerary and his hopes and fears about what will occur in the future (Rom 15:22–33; 1 Cor 16:5–9). In any case, we must ask the question: what is the function of the intended travelogue in Philippians? To answer this question requires that we examine the tone of the letter.

The Commendation of Two Models

The hortatory nature of Philippians is revealed in part by a disproportionate use of the imperative. Often Paul addresses the readers directly (1:27; 2:2–4, 12–15; 4:4–6, 8–9). Yet a different and peculiar pattern of exhortation emerges through the use of models, both positive and negative. The use of models is encouraged by the ancient teachers of rhetoric and occurs throughout Greek and Roman literature. Aristotle, for example, proposes the use of the paradigm either as a demonstration of a particular reality or a witness in support of a proposition (see *Rhet.* 2.20, 1393a, 1394a). Pseudo-Labanius offers the following as an illustration: "Always be an emulator, dear friend, of virtuous men. For it is better to be well spoken of when imitating good men than to be reproached by all men when following evil men" (*Epistolary Styles* 52). Examples of models abound in the hortatory letters of Seneca, Pliny, Isocrates, and the Socratics.[1] In Philippians, both Timothy and Epaphroditus are set forth as models, but in two very different ways.

2:19 I hope in the Lord Jesus to send Timothy to you soon that I also might be heartened by knowing your welfare. **20** I have no one like him who will be genuinely concerned about your situation. **21** All the others seek their

---

1. For further examples, see Johnson, "II Timothy and Polemic," 1–24; Fiore, *Personal Example*, 79–163; Kurz, "Kenotic Imitation," 103–26.

Travel Plans and Examples to Be Followed 65

own interests, and not the interests of Jesus Christ. 22 But you know Timothy's character, how like a son with a father he served with me in the cause of the gospel. 23 I hope, therefore, to send him to you as soon as I see how things go with me. 24 I have confidence in the Lord that also I myself will come soon.[a]

25 And I have considered[b] it necessary to send to you Epaphroditus, my brother and co-worker and fellow soldier, and your apostle[c] and servant of my need 26 since he has been longing for you all and was distressed because you had heard that he was sick. 27 And he was sick, near to death. But God had mercy on him, and not on him only but also on me lest I have grief on top of grief. 28 Therefore, I am sending him to you with haste, in order that seeing him again you may rejoice, and I may be less anxious. 29 Welcome him therefore in the Lord with all joy, and hold such people in honor, 30 because he came near to death on account of the work of Christ, risking his life, in order that he might supply what service you were not able to give me.

a. The expression "to you" is omitted from the more trustworthy manuscripts, such as P^{46}, B, D, and the majority of others. Apparently scribes have added the "to you" to make for a smoother read.

b. The aorist tense is likely an epistolary aorist, in which the writer takes the stance and time of his readers.

c. "Apostle" is used here in the sense of God's messenger without extraordinary status or authority. Epaphroditus was a messenger, only in the sense of bearing the Philippians' gift to Paul.

[2:19–24] Paul clearly wants to relate to the Philippians his desire to hear how they are faring. Timothy is sent for this purpose. He enjoys the status as co-sender of the letter (1:1), and in addition he is highly commended by Paul. Paul has no one like Timothy, who is genuinely concerned with the welfare of the Philippians. The others close to Paul in his imprisonment are interested only in themselves. The Philippians know Timothy's character, how he has labored in the cause of the gospel (see Acts 16:1–3; 20:3–6). He is of "like mind/soul" (*isopsychos*, 2:20) with the apostle. He has been like a son to Paul and is the obvious choice to visit Philippi since they also know and trust him. His role is depicted here much as a faithful emissary.

Paul's heartfelt approbation of Timothy indicates, however, that he is more than a trusted colleague. He models the type of life the apostle wants to see embodied in Philippi. He cares about others and exhibits in his own life the *phronēsis* that Paul has encouraged the Philippians to demonstrate (2:1–4). Two descriptions of Timothy even echo the Christ figure in the hymn: he looks not to his own interests but to the interests of others (2:20–21, cf. 2:4), and he "has served" (2:22; cf. 2:7) with Paul like a son.

[2:25–30] The same can be said for Epaphroditus, though not so much is known about him. His name would suggest that he was a Gentile whose parents had been devotees of Aphrodite, but he is mentioned nowhere else in the New Testament. Apparently he had become critically ill either on the way as he brought the gift from the Philippians or after he arrived at the place of Paul's imprisonment. In any case, his sickness was serious, and was exacerbated by his worry that the Philippians had heard and were concerned about his condition. Whether or not 2:26 indicates that Epaphroditus has been extremely homesick ("he has been longing for you all"), 2:27–28 plainly indicates that Paul is relieved of anxiety over Epaphroditus now that he has regained his health and is returning home. "Therefore I am sending him back as quickly as possible."

Yet Paul is concerned that Epaphroditus might not be received home with the proper respect he deserves. After all, he came near to death (*mechri thanatou,* 2:30) in order to bring the Philippians' gift to Paul. This Greek expression is found in only one other place in Paul's letters—in Phil 2:8 in connection with Christ's coming. He "became obedient as far as death" (*mechri thanatou*). Hawthorne, furthermore, notes that the participle *paraboleusamenos* ("risking his life," 2:30) may well imply "gambling his life" or "daringly exposing himself to danger," making it clear that Epaphroditus was no coward, but a courageous person, willing to take enormous risks, to aid a friend in need.[2]

On one level these words are meant to assure Epaphroditus of a warm welcome upon his return home, but on a deeper level, they commend Epaphroditus (like Timothy) as a model of the Christian life, one who hazards his life for the gospel. Particularly, the phrase "hold such people in honor" (2:29) lifts Epaphroditus and others like him into an exemplary role.[3]

Timothy and Epaphroditus may be worthy models for the Philippians, yet they are but imitators of the Christ of 2:6–11, who remains the generative model for all Christians. Christ's humiliation and in turn God's exaltation of him make it possible for Timothy and Epaphroditus (and as we shall later see, Paul also) to be exemplary characters for other believers.

[**2:24**] Paul adds a note in connection with Timothy's visit that he himself plans to visit the Philippians "soon." This of course is dependent on how his trial goes. "I have confidence in the Lord" (2:24) would suggest that any thought of imminent death was far from Paul's mind at this time. He fully expects to be freed and to return to serve the Philippians. Robert Funk, working on the notion that the letters were always surrogates for visits, has contended that the apostolic presence was extended through the mention of travel plans and an upcoming visit by the apostle.[4] The emphatic *autos* suggests that Tim-

---

2. Hawthorne, *Philippians,* 120.
3. See Kurz, "Kenotic Imitation," 113.
4. Robert W. Funk, "The Apostolic Parousia: Form and Significance," in *Christian History and Interpretation: Studies Presented to John Knox* (ed. William Reuben Farmer et al.; Cambridge: Cambridge University Press, 1967), 249–68.

othy's visit, as important as it is, does not serve as a substitute for the apostle's own presence among the Philippians.

3:1–4:3 Further Exhortations and Warnings

3:1–4a Call to Rejoice, Warning against Mutilators, the Church as True Circumcision

[3:1–2] At the beginning of chapter 3 we come to the first uneven seam in the letter that has led some commentators to find in Philippians a composition of three letters (see Introduction). The chapter begins with a Greek expression *to loipon*, which can mean "finally," and seems to anticipate a conclusion to the letter (so NRSV), though the apostle does not stop. The expression "rejoice in the Lord" (3:1) is repeated in 4:4. Joy in the Lord is the keynote of Paul's message to the Philippians.

The arguments in favor of multiple letters propose the same general divisions: three letters, each one written by Paul. We examine here an outline proposed by Collange, in the order in which he suggests the letters were written.[1] Letter A contains the passage 4:10–20 and is Paul's expression of thanksgiving for the gift that Epaphroditus brought him from the Philippians, a letter that has to do with the return of Epaphroditus, and the commendation of his work to the Philippians. Letter B incorporates several passages, first the section 1:1–3:1a, in which Paul announces the return of Epaphroditus and commends his work to the Philippians. This letter also addresses a church dispute (4:2–7) and contains the concluding greetings (4:21–23). In Letter C, Paul attacks his opponents (3:1b–4:1). This third letter concludes with 4:8–9 (and another "Finally"), its closing verses recalling the deep feelings and encouragement expressed in 4:1. We have argued in the Introduction that the letter reads better as a single letter.

We have to acknowledge, however, that 3:1–4 appears uneven, and leaves us with several questions: (1) How are we to translate *to loipon* (3:1)? (2) Why does Paul somewhat apologetically state that he is repeating himself (3:1b)? (3) Where should the paragraph break come—at the end of 2:30? at the end of 3:1a? at the end of 3:1b?

First, since Paul does not stop at the end of 3:1 and even uses *to loipon* again in 4:8, it seems wise to render the expression as a transition to something new in the letter ("in this connection," "moreover," or "therefore") rather than as "finally."[2] Second, the imperative to "rejoice in the Lord" of course repeats the

---

1. Collange, *Philippians*, 8–15.
2. Bauer and Danker, eds., BDAG, 603.

theme of "rejoicing" that occurs before and after this juncture in the letter (1:18; 2:17–18; 4:4, 10). Paul, however, would hardly seem to be apologizing for calling the people to "rejoice." The apostle could be referring to oral communications from Epaphroditus or Timothy as they repeated what he had written in the letter.[3]

Malherbe, however, has called attention to a standard feature in letters of this sort—an assurance to the readers that they are receiving nothing original, but time-tested, traditional counsel.[4] As Dio Chrysostom wrote, "Since I observe that it is not our ignorance of the difference between good and evil that hurts so much as it is our failure to heed the dictates of reason on these matters and to be true to our personal opinions, I consider it most salutary to remind men of this without ceasing" (*Dei cogn.* 17.2; cf. *Orations* 3.25–26; 3.14–15; Isocrates, *Nic.* 12; 40).

If 3:1b indeed announces a reminder, then "the same things" likely refers to the exhortation in 3:2 to "consider the dogs." Thus, the paragraph breaks would better come at the end of 2:30 and at the end of 3:1b. This arrangement eliminates the uneven seam and restores the integrity of the letter at this point (especially in light of 3:18).

3:1 Moreover,[a] my brothers and sisters,[b] be joyful in the Lord!
To write the same things to you is not troublesome for me, but it is a safe course for you.
2 Consider[c] the dogs! Consider the evil workers! Consider the mutilation![d] **3** For we are the circumcision, those who worship in the Spirit of God[e] and who boast in Christ Jesus, and put no confidence in the flesh, **4** although[f] I have reason for confidence in the flesh.

a. 3:1 begins with the expression *to loipon*, which is often rendered "finally," but also can be translated "moreover," or "therefore." It signals a transition to something new, often, though not exclusively, when it comes at the end of a literary work.

b. *Adelphoi* clearly includes women in the Philippian church.

c. As Kilpatrick has pointed out, the verb *blepō* when followed by a direct object in the accusative case does not take on the air of a warning.[5] Rather it directs one's attention to, or calls one to consider. Thus, here in 3:2 the mood is cautionary rather than hortatory.

d. Paul engages in a play on words in the Greek. "Mutilation" comes from the word *katatomē*, whereas "circumcision" comes from the Greek *peritomē*. Those who apparently insist on circumcision for non-Jewish converts are actually engaging in "mutilation." For a similar play on "circumcision," see Gal 5:12. Also all three terms used in 3:2 begin in the Greek with the letter kappa: *kynas, kakous ergatas, katatomē*.

---

3. See Furnish, "Philippians III," 86–88.
4. Malherbe, *Theorists*, 280.
5. Kilpatrick, "*Blepete*."

e. Some manuscripts (such as P[46]) omit *theou*, in which case the translation is "whose worship is spiritual" (NEB). However, sufficient manuscripts include *theou*, and the reading then without *theou* is to be explained by "accidental oversight."[6]

f. *Kaiper* is regularly followed by a participle, so *egō echōn*.

[3:3–4a] First, to claim the title "circumcision" for a church of uncircumcised Gentiles is to claim for them the promises made to Abraham. As Fowl notes,[7] Paul is no doubt drawing on Old Testament notions that circumcision of the heart must accompany physical circumcision (Deut 10:16; 30:6; Jer 4:4; 9:25–26). In Rom 2:25–29 the apostle makes the case, "A person is not a Jew who is one outwardly. . . . Rather a person is a Jew who is one inwardly, and real circumcision is a matter of the heart—it is spiritual and not literal." It would seem that the "dogs" were advocating circumcision as a necessity for Gentiles to secure their place in the covenantal community, whereas for Paul neither circumcision nor uncircumcision makes any difference with God whatsoever (cf. 1 Cor 7:19; Gal 5:6; 6:15).

Second, Paul claims for the church that it serves in the spirit of God. The participle *latreuontes* implies the carrying out of religious duties, especially of a cultic nature, and thus can be rendered as "worship."[8] The dative case indicates the manner in which the service is rendered ("in the Spirit of God"). The expression is related to the command "Rejoice in the Lord," for it is the spirit of God who enables the joy to be expressed.

To "boast in Jesus Christ and put no confidence in the flesh" is the third feature of the church, which distinguishes it from "the dogs." "Boast" is an interesting verb, which Paul may have taken from Jer 9:22–23 (see 1 Cor 1:31; 2 Cor 10:17) and certainly employs frequently. Of the thirty-seven uses of the verb in the New Testament, thirty-five occur in the Pauline letters. As Bultmann notes, the element of trust is primary to boasting so that self-confidence is radically excluded from boasting in God.[9] There is only one legitimate "boasting in God," namely "through our Lord Jesus Christ" (Rom 5:11). These Christians boast in Christ Jesus in whom they have put their trust, and specifically they put no confidence in the flesh.

"Flesh" is a critical notion for the apostle since it leads to extensive reflection on Paul's own experience. The Greek word for "flesh" (*sarx*) evidences a broad semantic range in the Pauline letters. In each instance the context, of course, becomes determinative of its meaning. It can denote simply being alive as a human being ("to remain in the flesh is more necessary for you," 1:24). Or it can denote humanity in its opposition to God (1 Cor 15:50; 2 Cor 5:16; 11:18). At times

---

6. Metzger, *Textual Commentary* (1971), 614.
7. Fowl, *Philippians*, 147–48.
8. Bauer and Danker, eds., BDAG, 587.
9. Rudolf Bultmann, "καυχάομαι, κτλ.," *TDNT*, 3:649.

"flesh" can act like an independent quasi-personal power to which one can orient one's life, as in the statement, "To set the mind on the flesh is death" (Rom 8:6). While "flesh" is not inherently evil, it can become the source for a long list of sins, as in Gal 5:19–21. Bultmann draws a careful distinction, when he notes that "flesh" can become the stage or the possibility for people's lives (as in Phil 1:24), or it can become the determinative norm according to which people orient their lives and presume to discover meaning. In the former case, it has no evil connotation, whereas in the latter case, it is the occasion for sinful self-delusion.[10] "To have confidence in the flesh" is the very opposite of "boasting in Christ Jesus."

Before moving to his own statement of faith, we need to take note of Paul's description of the church as those "who worship in the Spirit of God" and who boast in Christ Jesus." The "we" beginning 3:3 is in a strategic place in the sentence ("*We* are the circumcision"). Bassler notes that in the space of thirteen verses (2:19–3:1) the formula "in the Lord" occurs frequently and in so many different ways that "the modern reader tends to skip over it as pious filler."[11] Paul hopes "in the Lord Jesus" to send Timothy to Philippi (2:19), and he trusts "in the Lord" that he will also come soon (2:24). Meanwhile, the Philippians are to welcome Epaphroditus "in the Lord" (2:29) with all joy. They are to "rejoice in the Lord" (3:1). The Philippians are the true circumcision because they "worship in the Spirit of God and boast in Christ Jesus" (3:3). The two activities highlight both the source of strength for the community ("Spirit of God") and its ultimate orientation ("Christ Jesus").

What we are presented with in 3:2–3 is a pair of models, just as Timothy and Epaphroditus were models in the earlier section, only this set offers both positive and negative examples. On the one hand, there are the dogs, the evil workers, and the group who mutilate the flesh. On the other hand, there are the Philippians themselves who are the heirs of Abraham's promise, who worship in the spirit of God and boast in Christ Jesus. As Caird puts it, "The contrast is not between a Jewish worship which is external and Christian worship which is spiritual, but between a physical circumcision which is the symbol of obedience to a code of law and a circumcision of the heart, i.e., an inner transformation brought about by the gift of the Holy Spirit."[12]

3:4b–16 Paul's Story to Be Imitated

Mention of confidence in the flesh leads Paul to a self-reflection having to do with his own reasons for "boasting"—his heritage and his accomplishments. In

---

10. Bultmann, *Theology of the New Testament*, 1:239.
11. Jouette M. Bassler, *Navigating Paul: An Introduction to Key Theological Concepts* (Louisville, Ky.: Westminster John Knox, 2007), 40.
12. Caird, *Letters from Prison*, 134.

Further Exhortations and Warnings

the course of this meditation, he presents himself as a positive model for the readers, yet in a surprising way.

> **4b** If any person should think he has reason for confidence in the flesh, I have more: **5** circumcised on the eighth day; a member of the people of Israel; of the tribe of Benjamin; a Hebrew born of Hebrew parents; with regard to the law a Pharisee; **6** with regard to zeal a persecutor of the church; with regard to righteousness of the law, I was beyond reproach.[a]

a. *amemptos* ("beyond reproach") indicates Paul's faultlessness regarding the law, not that he lived a perfect life, free from sin.

[3:4b–6] Paul begins by listing his inherited credentials (3:4b–5d), followed by his achieved credentials (3:5e–6). He can claim circumcision in the precise manner required by the law (cf. Gen 17:12; 21:4; Lev 12:3). He was an Israelite by birth, from a favored tribe. The fact that he was "a Hebrew born of Hebrews" likely indicates that he spoke Aramaic as his native tongue. Born with these advantages of racial and religious heritage, Paul adds to them the practice of sincere piety and fanatical zeal. He was a Pharisee, which meant that he had lived with and under the law. According to Luke (Acts 5:34; 22:3), he studied as a disciple under the great Gamaliel, which would have given him status in rabbinical circles.

"With regard to zeal," he was "a persecutor of the church." "Zeal" can mean a number of things and is used widely in the New Testament. Here it seems to have the positive sense of ardor or passionate enthusiasm, and the proof of his zeal for the tradition of his ancestors is in his persecution of the church. Paul draws this connection between "being zealous" for the tradition of his ancestors and his persecution of the church also in Gal 1:13–14. That is to say, Paul's motivation in harassing the church was religious; in fact, it grew out of his study of the fathers and mothers of the faith. That may be why Paul does not apologize or seem at all remorseful for having been a persecutor of the church.

Finally, Paul acknowledges that with regard to righteousness he was beyond reproach. The word *amemptos* is rendered "blameless, faultless," though Paul does not claim that he was perfect or without transgression. He rather says that he has lived an exemplary life as a Jew ("as to righteousness concerning the law") and has taken advantage of the regular procedures which the law has provided to "maintain one's position within the covenant," to use Sanders's term.[13] By the law's standard of righteousness, Paul was beyond reproach. Yet this is not the manner in which he presents himself as a model.

---

13. E. P. Sanders, *Paul and Palestinian Judaism: A Comparison of Patterns of Religion* (Philadelphia: Fortress, 1977), 420.

3:7 Yet[a] whatever were for me assets,[b] these things I have counted as loss[b] because of Christ; and **8** what's more, I am counting all things as loss because of the surpassing value of knowing Christ Jesus my Lord. Because of him I have sustained the loss of all things and am counting them as rubbish,[c] in order that I may gain Christ **9** and be found in him, with no righteousness of my own, a righteousness based on law, but rather with the righteousness that comes through the faithfulness of Christ, a righteousness of God based on faith; **10** that I might know him and the power of his resurrection and[d] participation in his sufferings, being conformed to his death, **11** if somehow I may attain the resurrection of the dead.

a. The *alla*, as an adversative particle, indicates a strong contrast with what precedes, though it is omitted in some manuscripts (P[46], and Codex Alexandrinus).

b. The language comes from the world of bookkeeping. What once were considered as assets are now written off as losses.

c. The Greek word *skybala* denotes undesirable material that is subject to disposal: refuse, garbage, excrement, crud.

d. The prime manuscripts omit the article before "participation" (*koinōnia*), thus linking closely together the two nouns "power" and "participation."

[3:7] Having called attention to his inheritance and his achievements as an active Jew, Paul reaches the turning point in his theological pilgrimage. "Yet whatever were assets for me, I have counted as loss." Using the language of bookkeeping, he employs sharp words to describe how he feels about his heritage and his days as a Pharisee. They are regarded as "rubbish," "garbage." Items initially categorized as "gains" are abruptly shifted into the debit column, from an asset to a liability. But the loss in turn is just as quickly erased in favor of a new "gain," the incomparable worth of the knowledge of Christ.

[3:7–8] There is no hint that the past is regretted, as if it were sinful and something about which to be repenting. Paul's past, rather, is being reassessed. The verb *hēgeomai* ("count," "regard") occurs three times in the paragraph (3:7, 8 [twice]). "Paul characterizes this change in his life as a matter of change in perception—a cognitive shift."[14] What has occurred is a transformation in the way value is assigned, what matters and what does not matter.

This point is critical when speaking of Paul's "conversion." Philippians 3:4–11 does not relate the story of one who "converts" from one religion to another, as one might convert today from being a Christian to being a Muslim—that is, rejecting one religion for another. Paul still worships the God of Abraham and Sarah and still counts himself a Jew (2 Cor 11:22). In the Galatians account of his transformation (Gal 1:15–16) Paul uses the language of Jeremiah

14. Beverly R. Gaventa, *From Darkness to Light: Aspects of Conversion in the New Testament* (OBT; Philadelphia: Fortress, 1986), 33.

Further Exhortations and Warnings

(Jer 1:5) and the servant figure of Deutero-Isaiah (Isa 49:1, 6) to describe what occurred to him. This has led Krister Stendahl to refer to Paul's change as a "call," instead of a conversion.[15] In Phil 3:7–11, however, a definite change has occurred that is not paralleled in the prophets. What has been transformed is Paul's perception of the past. He views his pedigree and his religious accomplishments in a new light. He has experienced a transformation.

[3:8] The passage is remarkably christocentric in content. It is "the surpassing value of knowing Christ Jesus my Lord" that leads him to regard his past as "loss" (3:8). Expressions such as "gain Christ," "know Christ," and "be found in Christ" are frequent throughout the section. They express both the goal and the basis for Paul's new perception of himself. "Being incorporated into Christ" is the vantage point from which he now sees himself.

[3:9] Two moves are made in the text to define "knowing Christ." One has to do with being found in Christ "not having a righteousness of my own that comes from the law, but one that comes through the faithfulness of Christ, a righteousness from God based on faith." Despite all his reasons for boasting in the flesh, Paul rejects a righteousness of his own from the law. Instead, he claims an alien righteousness, a righteousness given by God. In the eschatological day, he anticipates being found rectified by a gift of God and not by some personal achievement of his own.

Somewhat debatable is the rendering of the phrase "through the faith of Christ" (NRSV margin) in 3:9 as opposed to "through faith in Christ" (NRSV). From the time of the Reformation, stress has been placed on how God's grace is received by humans—that is, by faith and not by works. The Reformation position has exercised a strong influence on English translations of the phrase *pistis Christou* (literally, "faith of Christ"). Is the *Christou* to be taken as an objective genitive and the phrase rendered as "through faith in Christ"? Or is the *Christou* to be taken as a subjective genitive and the phrase translated as "through the faith of Christ"? Syntactical arguments on either side of the debate tend to be inconclusive.

Richard Hays, however, argues convincingly that it makes more sense to read Paul as pitting a human activity (fulfilling the stipulations of the law) over against a divine activity (Christ's faithful obedience) than to read Paul as pitting one human activity (fulfilling the stipulations of the law) against another human activity (believing), especially since the divine activity lies at the heart of Paul's message.[16] Since there is an echo of the Christ hymn (Phil 2:6–11) in chapter 3, the phrase *dia pisteōs Christou* can serve as shorthand for the obedient

---

15. Krister Stendahl, *Paul among Jews and Gentiles and Other Essays* (Philadelphia: Fortress, 1976), 7–23.

16. Richard B. Hays, *The Faith of Jesus Christ: An Investigation of the Narrative Substructure of Galatians 3:1–4:11* (2d ed.; Grand Rapids: Eerdmans, 2002), 211.

self-surrender of Jesus—that is, to his faithful obedience unto death on a cross (2:8). Furthermore, if the subjective genitive is read, then one avoids duplication with the last phrase in 3:9, "the righteousness of God based on faith."

[3:10–11] The second move in the text is made in 3:10–11, where the knowledge of Christ is spelled out: "that I may know him and the power of his resurrection and participation in his sufferings, being conformed to him in his death, if somehow I may attain the resurrection of the dead." The sentence is complex and worthy of careful attention. The first *kai* ("and") in 3:10 is an explanatory (or an epexegetical) one, making the phrase "the power of his resurrection and participation in his sufferings" interpretive of "him." The sentence might read: "that I may know him, namely, the power of his resurrection and sharing in his sufferings." The two following clauses, one a participial construction ("being conformed . . .") and the other, a conditional clause ("if somehow I may attain . . ."), function adverbially to provide the circumstances for knowing Christ.

Moreover, the four expressions are structured in a chiastic fashion: a (resurrection), b (sufferings), b' (death), a' (resurrection).

that I might know him and the power of his resurrection	A
and participation in his sufferings,	B
being conformed to his death,	B'
if somehow I may attain the resurrection of the dead.	A'

These last two verses answer for the readers two interrelated, epistemological questions: What is it to *know Christ*? And *how* does one know Christ? The first question is answered by explaining that to know Christ is to know the power of his resurrection and to know participation in his sufferings. The second is answered by explaining that the knowing has to do with conformity to his death and the anticipation of the resurrection of the dead. The two answers obviously reinforce each other.[17]

The order of the terms in the phrase "the power of his resurrection and participation in his sufferings" sheds further light on the knowledge of Christ. One is more inclined to expect the opposite: first of sufferings and then resurrection, of Good Friday and then Easter, of anguish endured and then resolved. The textual sequence of resurrection and then suffering suggests that Christ's resurrection is known in the sharing of his sufferings. This is supported by the presence of the following present participle, which declares that the knowing of Christ has to do with a continual conformity to his death. Knowing Christ is not a matter of acquiring more adequate information about his life. Nor is it a question of developing a proper attitude toward him. As Karl Barth so point-

---

17. See Charles B. Cousar, *A Theology of the Cross: The Death of Jesus in the Letters of Paul* (OBT; Minneapolis: Fortress, 1990), 157–62.

Further Exhortations and Warnings 75

edly put it, "To know Easter means, for the person knowing, as stringently as may be: to be implicated in the events of Good Friday. . . . The way in which the power of Christ's resurrection works powerfully in the apostle is, that he is clothed with the shame of the cross."[18]

Paul is not offering a generalized explanation for all suffering; rather he speaks of the Philippians (and of himself) as those to whom suffering has been graciously given by God (Phil 1:29), as those who have been obedient to God in a world that does not tolerate such obedience. In the context of their suffering, they have come to know God in a new way.

[3:10] Two readings of 3:10 need to be avoided. Admittedly, mystical language is used in the text, but what is proposed is not a meditative reliving of Christ's passion. The focus is rather on participation with Christ in the midst of real-life sufferings and struggles of human existence. And second, the passage does not suggest that martyrdom is to be sought as a means of knowing Christ fully.[19] If martyrdom came for Paul, it came because he was serving the gospel, not because he sought it as a way to know Christ.

How one hears Paul's words regarding the knowledge of Christ as experienced through "the shame of the cross" is critical. We need to keep in mind that this word of the apostle's was written for a community that was about to undergo opposition (1:27–29), not for a group safely enjoying the fruits of protection and freedom. Furthermore, Paul does not condemn the law and circumcision, which were given by God. He simply sees himself in the light of the crucified and risen Jesus, and his new vantage point provides him a revolutionary self-understanding, in which he invites others to join him (3:15, 17).

Thus Paul offers himself as a model, not in terms of his achievements but as one who must live in conformity to the cross of Christ. Here is the secret offered by the letter. Christ has humbled himself, becoming obedient unto death, even death on the cross. The fact that the kenotic Christ has pioneered the way forward and has become the one to whom every knee bows makes it possible for Paul to become conformed to this Christ and himself to be a model for others.

3:12–16 Identification and Acceptance of Christ's Claim

Paul begins this section by saying that he has not attained the resurrection of the dead, but rather he presses on because Christ had made him his own. This leads him to want to know Christ and the power of his resurrection, even if it means sharing in his suffering by becoming like him in his death. Thus, he presses on toward the goal for the heavenly "call of God in Christ Jesus" (3:14).

---

18. Barth et al., *Philippians*, 103.
19. So Lohmeyer, *Kyrios Jesus*, 139.

3:12 Not that I have already attained it[a] or have already been made perfect; but I press on if I might also take hold of that which Christ Jesus[b] has taken hold of in me.[c] **13** Brothers and sisters, I do not[d] consider myself to have taken hold of it. But one thing I do: forgetting what lies behind and straining forward to what lies ahead, **14** I press on toward the goal for the prize of the upward call of God in Christ Jesus. **15** Let those of us who are mature think this same thing; and if anyone thinks differently, God will reveal this to you. **16** Only let us live up[e] to what we have attained.

a. Some Western manuscripts add "or already have been justified," which probably was the work of a "pious copyist who imagined that the Divine side of sanctification was left too much out of sight."[20] Metzger notes that the current reading is amply supported by a number of manuscripts.[21]

b. "Jesus" is omitted in several manuscripts, but included in the more important ones (P^{46}, Codices Alexandrinus, Vaticanus, as well as the majority of texts).

c. The verb *katalambanō*, which appears twice in v. 12 and once in v. 13, means "to make something one's own, to win, to attain." With *brabeiov* (v. 14), it is rendered "to win." In 3:12 the aorist passive is used, implying, "I have been taken hold of by Christ Jesus."

d. Some scribes evidently thought Paul was too modest in his protestations and substituted the word *oupō* ("not yet") for *ou*.[22]

e. Copyists apparently added words to clarify the meaning of *tō autō*. So the Textus Receptus adds *kanoni*, and the KJV reads, "Nevertheless, whereto we have already attained, let us walk by the same rule, let us mind the same thing."

[3:12-14] The bookkeeping imagery of 3:7-8 yields to the athletic imagery of 3:12-14. Three times Paul declares that he has not yet reached the goal. This becomes important in light of the earlier claim of what he has achieved in Judaism, that regarding the law he was "beyond reproach." Yet the present is an active time, focused and purposeful: "I press on to make it my own"; "straining forward to what lies ahead"; "I press toward the goal."

[3:14] After declaring the third time that he has not arrived, and that he is straining forward to what lies ahead, Paul declares that he is pressing toward the goal "unto the prize of the upward call of God in Christ Jesus" (3:14). What is this "prize of the upward call of God in Christ Jesus"? It is certainly not a reward for having run a good race. Rather it is a confirmation of the divine calling already received and which at the same time lies in the future. Caird comments, "The genitive is a genitive of definition: the prize consists in God's

---

20. Henry A. Kennedy, "Philippians," in *The Expositor's Greek Testament* (ed. W. Robertson Nicoll; 5 vols.; New York: Hodder & Stoughton, 1956), 3:457.

21. Metzger, *Textual Commentary* (1971), 615.

22. See ibid.

Further Exhortations and Warnings 77

invitation or call, and an 'above invitation' must be to a life which is to be lived above, i.e., in God's own presence."[23] Or as Bockmuehl puts it, "It is God who calls Paul in Christ, and who has already 'apprehended' Paul and made him his own. Paul's task is to reach out and grasp the prize for which he is already appointed."[24]

[3:15–16] Paul does not expect that all his readers will agree with him, yet he shows remarkable tolerance to those who differ. "Let those who are mature/perfect (*teleioi*) think this same way," he begins. But the apostle has just rejected any notion that he is perfect/mature (*teteleiōmai*) in 3:12. Could he be writing with irony here? Could there be a group in Philippi that claims for itself "perfection"? It is unlikely, in that nowhere else does he use *teleios* ironically, as well as the fact that he uses the term for himself. To be "mature" for Paul here means to run the race rather than to consider it over and won. Those Philippians who are conscious of still being in the race are the mature ones, and those who are still aware of running the race but who think differently from Paul on any point are invited to be open to God's "apocalypse" where their thinking may have gone awry. Paul trusts the Spirit to guide the church in the pattern of Christ, "that their love may increase more and more in all knowledge and insight and that they might discern the things that matter" (cf. 1:9–10). "Paul's tone is inclusive, not polemical."[25] "Only let us keep in step with the standard to which we have attained" (3:16).

It is significant that Paul's eschatology comes to the fore in 3:12–14. He mentions "the resurrection of the dead" in 3:11, which somehow he hopes to attain, but which sparks the disclaimer in 3:12 that the resurrection has been already achieved. Paul has been united with the suffering Christ, but he awaits the resurrection of the dead (cf. Rom 6:1–11; 1 Cor 15:20–28). There is an "already" to Paul's faith. He has been united with Christ; however, he awaits the fulfillment, the "not yet," represented here by "the resurrection of the dead." What lies behind cannot distract him; it is considered "loss." What eagerly engages him is "the upward call of God in Christ Jesus."

3:17–19 Take Note of the "Enemies of the Cross"

3:17 Brothers and sisters, join in imitating me and observe those who walk according to the example that you have in us. 18 For many, as I was saying to you and now say, with tears, walk as enemies of the cross of Christ. 19 Their end is destruction; their God is the belly; and their glory is in their shame; they mind earthly things.

---

23. Caird, *Letters from Prison*, 143.
24. Bockmuehl, *Philippians*, 223.
25. Ibid., 225.

Paul is blunt in his statement to the Philippians. "Join in imitating me." He presents himself as a model, just as Timothy and Epaphroditus were models. However, one need not take this as an arrogant statement. We remember that the Philippian community had no precedents. They had no historical direction, no written gospels, and thus they looked to individuals like Paul, Timothy, and Epaphroditus for moral and spiritual guidance. Furthermore, we remember that in the ancient world students were expected to imitate their teachers. Dio Chrysostom, reflecting on the relation of Socrates to Homer, wrote,

> Whoever really follows anyone surely knows what that person was like, and by imitating his acts and words, he tries as best he can to make himself like him. But that is precisely, it seems, what the pupil does—by imitating his teacher and paying heed to him he tries to acquire his art.[26]

But why would Paul call on the Philippians to *join* in imitating him? Some commentators have taken this expression (*symmimētai mou*) to mean that the readers are to "join him" in imitating Christ, that they are to be "imitators with me," rather than being "imitators of me." Paul's logic, however, seems the same as in 1 Cor 11:1, where he urges the Corinthians to "be imitators of me, as I am of Christ." Just as Timothy and Epaphroditus have been exemplary models whom the Philippians have been encouraged to follow, so Paul himself is such an example.[27]

What in Paul's autobiography is to inform the mind of these readers? In what sense are they to be imitators of him? First, Paul has made knowing Christ the center of his life, and it has made a claim on him that has forced a reassessment of all other claims. Second, he has discovered that knowing Christ involves participation in his sufferings and death and anticipation of his resurrection from the dead. Third, knowing Christ remains for Paul a future expectation, a goal to be aimed at, a finish line to be pressed toward. It is neither his personal experience nor his achievements that is prominent, rather his desire to know Christ. Others have followed the same example Paul has followed, "who live according to the same pattern (*typos*)." They are to be trusted and followed. Thus, Paul is not the only one the Philippians can emulate.

At the same time he has told them about some who are "enemies of the cross of Christ, whose end is destruction, whose god is their belly, who glory in their shame, who set their mind on earthly things" (3:18–19). This group is opposed to the gospel and hardly represents a model to be followed.

The practice of comparing antithetical models was a widely employed exercise recommended in the Greco-Roman schools as a rhetorical device. It had

---

26. Discourse 55.4, 5. See further statements in Willis Peter De Boer, *The Imitation of Paul: An Exegetical Study* (Kampen: Kok, 1962); Kurz, "Kenotic Imitation," 103–26; Ernest Best, *Paul and His Converts* (Edinburgh: T&T Clark, 1968), 59–72.

27. Hooker, "Philippians," 534.

Further Exhortations and Warnings 79

the advantage of highlighting virtuous deeds and placing them in comparison to the misdeeds. Already we have seen in 1:15–18 the antithetical reactions to Paul's imprisonment. Here (3:18–19) several qualities characterize this group, who are called "enemies of the cross":

- Their end is destruction.
- Their god is the belly.
- Their glory is in their shame.
- They mind (*phronountes*) earthly things.

That they are labeled "enemies of the cross" hints at a connection with groups in Corinth (1 Cor 1:10–2:5) or Galatia (Gal 6:12), but either connection is tenuous, to say the least. "Their god is the belly" might be a metonym for an unbridled appetite, or possibly for its opposite, a preoccupation with regulations about eating and drinking. Paul hardly seems to be contending against a specific group in Philippi, but rather he is presenting a model not to be followed, an example of how they should not let their minds be shaped. The connections with other models in the letter are striking. While this group is described as "enemies of the cross," Christ is obedient unto death, even "death on a cross" (Phil 2:8); Epaphroditus comes near to death for the work of Christ (2:30), and Paul seeks to share Christ's sufferings and be conformed to his death (3:10). For "the enemies of the cross" the end is destruction, whereas Christ's end is his universal lordship (2:9–11), and Paul's goal is "the upward call of God in Christ" (3:14). Finally, while the mind of this group is oriented toward "earthly things," the Philippian community is to be shaped by Christ's story (2:5) and by Paul's story (3:15).

Very little is told us about the "enemies of the cross," and Paul does not engage them theologically as he does the opponents in Galatia or Corinth. Thus, rather than discovering in 3:18–19 the depiction of actual opponents in Philippi, who are a real threat to the Christians there, it is better to see in the "enemies of the cross" a group whom Paul discerns as a negative model. And yet since he mentions them "with tears," they must represent a real group. As Jerry Sumney puts it, "It is a didactic section with a hortatory intent."[28]

3:20–21 The Church's Heavenly Citizenship

3:20 But our commonwealth is in heaven, from which we also eagerly await a Savior, the Lord Jesus Christ, **21** who will transform the body of our humiliation,[a] conformed to the body of his glory according to the power that enables him to bring all things under his control.

28. Jerry L. Sumney, *"Servants of Satan," "False Brothers" and Other Opponents of Paul* (JSNTSup 188; Sheffield: Sheffield Academic Press, 1999), 182.

a. The majority of manuscripts add *eis to genesthai auto*, but it is unnecessary and is omitted from the major manuscripts, such as Sinaiticus, Alexandrianus, and Bezae.

Several commentators have found in 3:20–21 a pre-Pauline hymn or creedal fragment of six lines, based primarily on the parallels between 3:20–21 and 2:6–11. John Reumann casts "a somewhat tentative vote" in favor of such a hymn.[29] There are several linguistic connections between 2:6–11 and 3:20–21, suggesting that the letter might contain two separate hymns from the same tradition. Lincoln isolates nine expressions from 3:20–21 that are paralleled in 2:6–11.[30] The argument goes that since the first set of terms is found in what is generally thought to be a hymn, then the second and similar set also must derive from a hymn from the same conceptual context.

Lincoln, however, argues persuasively against 3:20–21 representing a pre-Pauline hymnic formula.[31] As we have seen several times, Paul has drawn on the language of 2:6–11 throughout the letter, and there is good reason to think that he employs the language of 2:6–11 here to depict what the church is and should be. Is there not more reason to assume that material from the first hymn has been skillfully used to produce a correspondence that suits Paul's intention at this point in his argument than that 3:20–21 comes from a different hymnic fragment?

Not only do the "enemies of the cross" serve as a foil for Paul's story, but they also function as the background for the statements about the nature of the Philippian community. They focus on "earthly things," whereas "our citizenship is in heaven." "Their end is destruction," whereas our end is the transformed "body of his glory." They have no eschatological expectation, whereas the Christian community awaits the advent of the Savior, who is the Lord Jesus Christ.

[3:20–21] The language of 3:20–21 is striking. First, "our commonwealth is in heaven." The term "commonwealth" would have carried plenty of clout in the first-century world of Philippi, with its political aura and its imperial pride. This is the only appearance of the word in the New Testament. It denotes a colony of foreigners, whose allegiance is, in this instance, not to Rome, but to God in heaven. "Commonwealth" is a dynamic term. Perhaps one way of expressing the connotation is the admittedly awkward rendering, "For our state and constitutive government is in heaven."[32] The confession of Christ as Savior and the commitment of those whose loyalties are (the present tense: *hyparchei*) in the heavenly commonwealth separate them from those whose

---

29. John Reumann, "Philippians 3:20–21, a Hymnic Fragment?" *NTS* 30 (1980): 594–609, following Lohmeyer, *Kyrios Jesus*, 156–62, and Erhardt Güttgemanns, *Der leidende Apostel und sein Herr: Studien zur paulinischen Christologie* (Göttingen: Vandenhoeck & Ruprecht, 1966), 240–47.
30. Lincoln, *Paradise*, 87–89.
31. Ibid.; cf. also Hooker, *Adam to Christ*, 20–22.
32. Lincoln, *Paradise*, 100.

Further Exhortations and Warnings 81

allegiance is elsewhere. Unlike the citizens of Rome, whose commonwealth is in Rome, the Philippian Christians eagerly await a Savior who is Christ the Lord. The Romans testified that Caesar (Claudius) is "Savior of the world."[33] Oakes concludes his study by saying, "In the first century AD, the one whom most people would see as saving in accordance with his power to subject all things to himself was the Emperor."[34] The confession of Jesus Christ as Savior is thus a subversive statement and no doubt the primary reason the Philippian Christians were subjected to persecution (1:27–30).

The awaiting of the Lord Jesus Christ has two critical elements to it. First, it entails the transformation of our body of humiliation, being conformed to the body of his glory. The continuity between now and then is the "body" (the person); however, it undergoes a transformation from being one of humiliation to being the body of the divine glory. As in 1 Cor 15:51, a "change" occurs. Christ's "resurrection," though not specifically mentioned in this passage, effects a complete change, making our humanity conformable to his divine glory. The language used reflects that of Phil 2:6–11. Just as Christ takes the "form" (*morphē*) of a slave, so he makes our humanity "conformable" (*symmorphon*) to his glory. Further, Christ has "emptied himself" (*etaipeinōsen*) in his act of obedience that our body of "humiliation" (*tapeinōseōs*) might be transformed.

Second, this transformation occurs through the cosmic power of God given to Christ, "the power that enables him to make all things subject to himself" (3:21). This notion may have come from Isa 45:20–25, which is cited in Phil 2:10–11 and where God is called "Savior," or possibly from Ps 110:1, a coronation psalm understood by Christians to have been said about Christ ("The LORD says to my lord, 'Sit at my right hand until I make your enemies your footstool"; cf. Matt 22:44; 26:64; Mark 12:36; 14:62; Luke 20:42–43; 22:69; Acts 2:34–35; Rom 8:34; 1 Cor 15:25; Eph 1:20; Col 3:1; Heb 1:3, 13; 8:1; 10:12); or possibly from Ps 8:6 ("You have given them dominion over the works of your hands; you have put all things under their feet"). In any case, the resurrection "is not seen as an isolated event, but as the last act in the drama of cosmic redemption."[35] The same power that brings all things under Christ's divine sway transforms our bodies of humiliation to conform to the body of his divine glory. In the face of the Roman demands upon Christians, they can trust that "any humiliation an empire might place on the bodies of the faithful will be transformed and redeemed by the power of the resurrected Christ."[36]

---

33. See Oakes, *Philippians*, 140.
34. Ibid., 145.
35. Caird, *Philippians*, 149.
36. Fowl, *Philippians*, 175.

4:1–3 Appeals to Steadfastness and Unity

4:1 So then, my brothers and sisters, whom I love and yearn for, my joy and my crown, stand firm in the Lord, beloved ones. 2 I beg Euodia and I beg Syntyche to be of the same mind in the Lord. 3 And indeed, I ask you, trusted companion,[a] to help[b] these women, for they have struggled beside me in the work of the gospel, together with Clement and the rest of the co-workers, whose names are written in the book of life.[c]

a. Some have taken this as a name, Syzygus, since it can mean "joiner together." Is it a reference to one of Paul's co-workers, such as Timothy (Collange) or Luke (Fee) or Epaphroditus (Lightfoot), or Paul's wife (Clement of Alexandria)? Or could it refer to the whole church (Barth)?[37] No doubt Paul's original audience could decipher the allusion, even if we can't.

b. The exhortation to "help" Euodia and Syntyche is in the present participle, which may imply that they are already on the road to reconciliation; "continue to help them."

c. "The book of life" is a familiar term both in the Old Testament (Exod 32:32; Ps 69:28; Dan 12:1) and the New Testament (Rev 20:12–15).

The larger section (3:1–4:3) closes with exhortations founded on the positive and negative models that have been developed. The conjunction *oste* ("therefore," "and so") indicates the close link between the models and the exhortations. The latter are not merely tacked on to the end of the letter, but grow out of the life of the models and the invitation to the readers to imitate the models. The Philippians are addressed as family members, reminiscent of the warm and affectionate beginning of the letter (1:3–11). Furthermore, they are called "beloved and yearned for," Paul's "joy and crown." The initial exhortation is that they "stand firm in the Lord." This apparently is a reminder of 1:27, where the Philippians are told to "stand firm in one Spirit," as "soul mates," contending for the faith of the gospel. As they are faced with opposition, they are to keep ranks and not to divide into warring factions. So at the end of the letter, Paul reminds them again to "stand firm."

[4:2–3] This general call to "stand firm" is followed by a direct word to two women in the church who apparently have had or currently are having a disagreement over an issue or problem in the church. Since it is rare that Paul singles out individuals by name, some commentators have highlighted these women as the cause for Paul's writing the letter and contend that they represent two factions in a divided church. Peterlin, for example, argues that Euodia and Syntyche were prosperous patronesses within the church and that they have divided over the issue of providing financial support for Paul's ministry.[38] The

37. See Collange, *Philippians*, 153; Fee, *Philippians*, 293; Lightfoot, *Philippians*, 158; Barth et al., *Philippians*, 120.
38. Peterlin, *Disunity*, 101–32.

letter is written fundamentally to address the issue of church support. There is no indication, however, that Euodia and Syntyche were deacons or patrons within the church, or that financial concerns were a major reason for Paul's writing the letter. He appropriately thanks them for the gifts sent to him in his ministry, but nothing is hinted at in his thank-you that the church is divided over having sent the gifts.

Cynthia Briggs Kittredge likewise argues that the letter leads up to 4:2, but contends that the mention of the two women following the affectionate language of 4:1 creates an "insider" and "outsider" relationship, in which Paul urges the women to "be of the same mind in the Lord."[39] "In 4:3, Paul addresses someone else in the second person and instructs that person to become involved with both women."[40] Thus, the division is not between the two women but between Paul and the two women. Mary Rose D'Angelo goes so far as to argue that Euodia and Syntyche were missionary partners, with a sexual dimension.[41]

Each of these interpretations loses sight of the fact that Paul speaks of these two women as persons who have struggled alongside him and Clement in the cause of the gospel. He urges them to be "of the same mind in the Lord," the same petition he has asked the entire church to demonstrate (2:2). Like Clement, their names are inscribed in "the book of life." Furthermore, though citing him, Kittredge fails to respond to the observation of Marshall regarding the usual practice in a letter like this of naming friends, while leaving enemies nameless.[42]

Who is this person whom Paul asks to "help these women"? "Syzygus," yet there is no one ever mentioned by that name, either in the New Testament or in Greek inscriptions. Other suggestions have included Timothy, Luke, Silas, and Epaphroditus. Lightfoot makes a good case for Epaphroditus since he would be the bearer of the letter and present in the community.[43] The present tense of the imperative "help" might suggest that these women had already begun to heal their differences and needed little help in the reconciliation process.

While there is precious little we know about Euodia, Syntyche, Clement, and those whose names are written in the book of life, and though we cannot be sure who the "true companion" is who is asked to assist these two colleagues with their differences, we can be sure that there is no major split within the church. He simply urges them to be of the same mind "in the Lord," the same exhortation he has asked of the whole church (2:2). All these people have engaged in the work of the gospel and have joined Paul in the spread of the good news.

---

39. Cynthia Briggs Kittredge, *Community and Authority: The Rhetoric of Obedience in the Pauline Tradition* (HTS 45; Harrisburg, Pa.: Trinity, 1998), 90–108.
40. Ibid., 106.
41. Mary Rose D'Angelo, "Women Partners in the New Testament," *JFSR* 6 (1990): 65–86.
42. Marshall, *Enmity*, 35–67.
43. Lightfoot, *Philippians*, 148–49.

4:4–23 Closing

Paul concludes the issue concerning the differences between Euodia and Syntyche by acknowledging that their names, together with the names of the other co-workers, are written in the book of life. They are not outsiders, but members of the family of faith. This then leads him to return to the theme of joy, which has so dominated this letter.

4:4–9 Final Exhortations

4:4 Rejoice in the Lord always. Again, I say, rejoice. **5** Let your gentleness be known to all people. The Lord is near. **6** Do not be anxious about anything, but in every situation, by prayer and petition, with thanksgiving, let your requests be known to God. **7** And the peace of God, which transcends all understanding, will guard your hearts and your minds in Christ Jesus. **8** Finally,[a] brothers and sisters,[b] whatever is true, whatever is noble, whatever is just, whatever is pure, whatever is lovely, if there is anything of virtue or worthy of praise, ponder[c] these things. **9** And the things that you have learned, and have received and heard and have seen in me, continue to do,[c] and the God of peace will be with you.

    a. *To loipon* could be translated "therefore," although since Paul does begin to end the letter here, it seems better to render it "finally."
    b. The NRSV loses the family character of this expression by translating it "beloved."
    c. Both imperatives are in the present tense.

[4:4] We have encountered the word "joy" so many times in this letter that it has to be considered a major theme of the epistle. Paul begins by saying that he prays for the Philippians "with joy" (1:4) because of their participation with him in the gospel (1:18, 25; 2:2, 17–18, 28–29; 3:1; 4:1, 10). They are "his joy and crown" (4:1). As he concludes the letter, he enjoins them to "rejoice in the Lord," and then repeats himself, "Again, I say, rejoice" (4:4).

Three features mark the theme of joy in Philippians. First, joy is highly paradoxical; it appears when it is least expected—in times of trial and struggle (cf. Rom 5:1–5). In this letter, "joy" is spoken of from a person in prison to people who are about to undergo persecution. Barth speaks of joy in Philippians as "a defiant 'Nevertheless!' which Paul sets like a full stop against the Philippians' anxiety."[1] Calvin earlier wrote, "It is a rare virtue that when Satan endeavors to irritate us by the bitterness of the cross so as to make God's name unpleasant

---

    1. Barth et al., *Philippians*, 120.

to us, we rest in the taste of God's grace alone, so that all annoyances, sorrows, anxieties, and griefs are sweetened."[2]

Second, joy is an eschatological reality. Often used in conjunction with hope (e.g., Rom 12:12; 15:13), joy is "the Christian's relatedness to the future."[3] The readers have a reason to rejoice because their "commonwealth is in heaven" (3:20) and because "the Lord is near" (4:5). And "he will transform the body of our humiliation to be conformed to the body of his glory" (3:21).

Third, joy entails mutuality. One does not experience joy alone, but in the company of God's people. The imperative "rejoice in the Lord always" immediately follows Paul's words regarding Euodia and Syntyche, that they have "one mind" because they have struggled with him and with Clement and the rest of his co-workers in the cause of the gospel. The phrase "in the Lord" (4:1, 2, 4) carries ecclesial as well as christological import. Joy is the experience of deep delight shared between parties (as in 2:17–18).

The exhortations to "stand firm" and to the women "to be of one mind" and to the whole community to "rejoice in the Lord always" are followed by yet other charges. "Let your gentleness be known to everyone" (4:5, NRSV). Or is it "your moderation" (KJV), or "your magnanimity" (NEB), or "your consideration of others" (REB)? The Greek adjective *epieikes* is defined as "not insisting on every right of letter of the law or custom; yielding; gentle; kind; courteous; tolerant."[4] Thus in 4:4 it describes a forbearing spirit, a gentleness, whereby one makes allowances despite facts that might suggest a different reaction.

[4:5–6] In the midst of the exhortations comes this short statement: "The Lord is near" (4:5), which provides a theological underpinning for Paul's instructions. Does the "nearness" of the Lord refer to God's spatial nearness, reflected in the psalms, such as Ps 34:18 and Ps 145:18, which speak of the brokenhearted and God's presence to those who call upon him? Or does the "nearness" refer to temporal nearness? In light of the eschatological emphasis of the New Testament community, the stress seems to fall more likely on the second advent of the Lord (cf. 1 Cor 16:22 and, in particular, Phil 3:20). The return of Jesus makes possible the rejoicing of the community as well as their demonstration of Christian gentleness. Still another exhortation follows. "Do not worry about anything, but in everything by prayer and supplication with thanksgiving, let your requests be made known to God" (4:6). Here the apostle is saying to the Philippians to let go of their burdensome worries, their anxieties over which they have no control, and instead to pray to God. Let their requests be known to God, and do so with thanksgiving.

---

2. John Calvin, *The Epistles to the Galatians, Ephesians, Philippians, and Colossians* (Grand Rapids: Eerdmans, 1965), 267.
3. Bultmann, *Theology of the New Testament*, 2:239.
4. Bauer and Danker, eds., BDAG, 371.

Being free of anxieties is therefore not something one can master oneself. Paul is not a Stoic. He does not offer a neat pattern whereby one can overcome cares and troubles. Because the Lord is near, believers can pray to God and lay their requests before him. Even in a world where they have to live amid opposition and hostility, they can cast their cares on God and can do so with thanksgiving, knowing that God will answer their petitions. As Barth comments, "The accent of the sentence lies not on the fact that they are to worship and pray, nor on the fact that they are to lay their *aitēmata* ('troubles') before God, but on the fact that they are to do both these things with thanksgiving (*meta eucharistias*)."[5]

[4:7] The conclusion of all this is that "the peace of God will guard" their hearts and minds in Christ Jesus. By "peace" the apostle seems to imply the Hebrew concept *shalom*, expressed in the familiar Mosaic/Aaronic benediction: "The LORD bless you and keep you; the LORD make his face to shine upon you; the LORD lift up his countenance upon you and give you *peace*" (Num 6:24–26). Certainly here in Philippians peace differs markedly from the *pax Romana*, which brought considerable anguish and strife in the effort to secure the roads of the empire and make the seas safe for travel. God's peace is far more than the absence of conflict; it even exceeds human imagination. The Greek verb *phrourēsei* is a military word, suggesting "standing guard over." "By union with Christ, in obedience to his authority and submission to his will, they will discover the security of their lives as they are assured of divine protection, 'God's Peace.'"[6]

[4:8–9] While some of the virtues that are made the objects of reflection in 4:8 may have peculiarly Pauline connotations ("just," "true"), they are widely used in the popular philosophical traditions of the day and carry nothing uniquely Christian about them. Was Paul trying to show that the Christian ethic is in many ways no different from pagan culture at its best? This seems unlikely, in that in 4:9 they are to "do" the things they have seen in Paul, who embodies the Christian message for them. Unlike the miscellaneous collection of exhortations at the beginning of chapter 4, those appearing in 4:8–9 are more structured and eloquently presented:

> Whatever is true,
> whatever is noble,
> whatever is just,
> whatever is pure,
> whatever is lovely,
> whatever is commendable,
>> if there is anything of virtue,
>> if there is anything worthy of praise,
>>> continue to ponder these things.
>
>   (4:8)

---

5. Barth et al., *Philippians*, 122–23.
6. Martin, *Philippians*, 157.

> What things you have learned, and
> > you have received, and
> > you have heard, and
> > you have seen in me,
> > > continue to do these things.
> > > > (4:9)

The paralleling of the two present imperatives ("ponder" and "do") indicates that the two verses are to be read together. Particularly in 4:9 the distinctively Christian teaching, tradition, spoken word, and example are set before the Philippians. They are urged not to worry, but to pray. "In everything let your requests be made known to God" (4:6).

Paul thus begins with a strong antidote to anxiety—praying with thanksgiving—and concludes this section of exhortations with an affirmation: that "the God of peace will be with you." The peace—that is, the blessings and promises that come from God—will be assured because God himself will be present with his people. Paul expresses thanks for their generosity to him, not only for the gift borne by Epaphroditus, but for their spirit of giving. The Philippians could be singled out among the various Pauline communities for their giving. They had sent gifts not once but twice during the initial missionary effort in Macedonia, and the apostle takes the opportunity to say "thank you."

And yet the thank-you has always presented a puzzle to interpreters, leading Lohmeyer in describing this section to coin the expression *"danklose Dank"* ("thankless thanks").[7] Two factors have led to this perplexing conclusion. One is the location of the thanksgiving. It comes so late in the letter that it seems tacked on, as if Paul were saying, "Oh, yes, by the way, thanks for your gift." The other factor is that Paul is not very effusive in his words of thanks. He never uses the word *eucharisteō*. Was Paul actually embarrassed to receive such a gift? He seems to write more about his ability to cope amid difficult circumstances (4:11–13) and his own sense of independence than he does to express thanks.

4:10–20 The Matter of Giving and Receiving

4:10 I rejoice in the Lord greatly that now, at last, your concern for me has blossomed anew; indeed, you were concerned, but you lacked the opportunity to express it. 11 Not that I am saying this because of my need, for I have learned to be content in the circumstances that I find myself. 12 I know what it is to be humbled, and I know what it is to have plenty. In any and in all situations I have learned the secret both of being well fed and of going hungry, both of having plenty and of being in need. 13 I am

---

7. Lohmeyer, *Briefe*, 178.

sufficient for all things through the one[a] who strengthens me. 14 Only it was good of you that you shared my afflictions.

15 You Philippians also know that in the beginning of the gospel when I came from Macedonia, no church shared in the matter of giving and receiving, except you only. 16 And when I was in Thessalonica you sent to[b] my need more than once. 17 Not that I desire your gifts, but I desire the fruit which abounds to your credit. 18 I have received full payment and more than enough, having received from Epaphroditus the gifts you sent, a fragrant offering, an acceptable sacrifice, pleasing to God. 19 And my God will fully satisfy every need of yours according to his riches in glory in Christ Jesus. 20 To our God and Father be glory forever and ever. Amen.

a. A number of manuscripts[8] include "Christ" in order to clarify who is the one who strengthens Paul. It is clearly a scribal addition.

b. The preposition *eis* is lacking in several manuscripts, as if the scribes wrote "you sent me what I needed" (P[46] and Alexandrianus).

[4:10] First, let us consider the location of this "thanksgiving." It is true that Paul has not written much about the gift prior to 4:10, and yet he has said a great deal about the Philippians' participation with him in the cause of the gospel. The entire prayer of thanksgiving (1:3–11) is devoted to his appreciation of their joining him in "the defense and confirmation of the gospel" (1:7). Despite his imprisonment Paul begins his letter by defining the nature of the Philippian partnership with him and reporting on the gospel's progress. The position of Paul's thanksgiving in the letter is consistent with their financial support of him. The concern about the lateness is a judgment based on a modern, Western criterion that the thanksgiving should come earlier in the letter, a criterion that is in fact inappropriate for Hellenistic letters.

Paul begins his thank-you by acknowledging that the Philippians' gift to him has given him great joy. He is pleased that they have joined him in the cause of the gospel. Here in 4:10 Paul returns to the theme of the letter, and it is here that his joy has resulted from the sharing, which the Philippians undertook. This is the only appearance of *megalōs* in the New Testament, and Peterman notes, "Though Paul never seems shy of expressing his feelings, this is the only place where he qualifies his own experience of joy."[9] Furthermore, he expresses his grounds for joy. Though there has apparently been an uncharacteristic gap since the Philippians' last gift has been given, he rejoices that at last their concern

8. For example, Uncial Codices such as Sinaiticus (corrected), Claromontanus, Athous Laurae, et al.; Miniscules 81, 1241, et al.; other witnesses: the Byzantine family, early Greek Lectionaries, et al.; evidence from the church fathers: Origen, Eusebius, Basil, Cyril-Jerusalem, Gregory-Nyssa, Didymus, Chrysostom, Jerome, et al.

9. Peterman, *Gift*, 128.

(*phronein*) for him has blossomed again, though heretofore they were hindered in sending him a gift.

Lest it look as though he needs a gift, he quickly moves to say that he is not referring to his need, for he has learned in whatever situation he finds himself to be content (*autarkēs*). The term Paul uses for himself is characteristic of Greek philosophers, and particularly the Stoics, who believed that they could achieve a certain self-sufficiency, an inner freedom independent of the ups and downs of life. Seneca wrote, "The wise man is sufficient unto himself for a happy existence" (*Lucil.* 9.23). Whether or not Paul is dependent on the Stoics for his language, it makes for a marvelous confession of faith: "I can do all things through him who strengthens me" (meaning either God or Jesus). Paul's freedom and inner strength are not dependent on the mastery of the self, as with the Stoics, but on the grace of God.

[4:11–13] Why does Paul do little more than acknowledge the gifts brought to him by Epaphroditus, as well as the gifts given him while he was in Corinth (2 Cor 11:7–9) and while he was in Thessalonica (Phil 4:16)? He plays down his need (4:11–12) and makes it clear that he did not request the gifts (4:17). Caird makes the suggestion that Paul faces a delicate situation.[10] On the one hand, he wants to express his profound and genuine gratitude for gifts, which he knows came out of "their extreme poverty" (2 Cor 8:2). On the other hand, if he overstates his thanksgiving, the Philippians may think he is in worse straits than he is and feel guilty for not helping him sooner or more generously than they did. Caird thus contends that Paul steers his way through the traps of a thank-you, saying enough but not too much, expressing gratitude but not asking for more.

A more likely explanation for the apparently enigmatic expression of thanks, however, emerges from the ancient social conventions of friendship. While it was morally commendable to give to a friend without thought of return, the recipient of a gift was under a heavy responsibility to reciprocate with at least the same, if not more than what one received. Aristotle went so far as to suggest that one not make friends if one were not in a position to return the friend's favors (*Eth. nic.* 8.13.9).

[4:15–19] Several expressions in 4:15–19 are characteristic of the friendship motif ("no church *shared* with me *in the matter of giving and receiving*, except you alone," 4:15). Paul would not be able to reciprocate to the Philippians, but he would entrust God to discharge his responsibility (4:19). Marshall rightly concludes[11] that Paul is drawing upon familiar notions of friendship to acknowledge the recent gift and to express his gratitude. Rather than pointing to tension or embarrassment on Paul's part over the gift, the language implies

---

10. Caird, *Letters from Prison*, 152.
11. Marshall, *Enmity*, 163–64.

the opposite. It reflects a warm and lasting relationship. He not only receives the gift gladly as a sign of their continued concern, but also recalls the mutual exchange of services and affection that he had shared in their past. Though he himself cannot reciprocate in kind, he is more than confident that God would more than make good of the gift out of, and in a manner befitting, his boundless wealth in Christ Jesus (v. 19).

Paul operates out of the notion of social reciprocity; only for him the gospel controls that reciprocity. He acknowledges that the Philippians have given him "a fragrant offering, a sacrifice acceptable and pleasing to God." He has been "paid in full." And yet, Paul is a more significant giver, in that "he gives something of far greater value and more costly: he gives himself and the gospel."[12]

4:21–23 Greetings and Benediction

21 Greet every saint in Christ Jesus. All the brothers and sisters with me send their greetings. 22 All the saints greet you, especially those of Caesar's household.

23 The grace of the Lord Jesus Christ be with your spirit.

The letter concludes with the typical sending of greetings, only this time specific mention is made of the sending of greetings from the saints of "the emperor's household," apparently a reference to those of the imperial guard who have received the gospel (1:13). It does not necessarily refer to the emperor's family in Rome, but to the large number of slaves and freedmen, and soldiers who served the emperor throughout the provinces. It would not have been easy for Paul to designate these people as "saints," but then it would have been difficult for those in Caesar's employment to acknowledge Jesus as Lord. And yet "the saints" send greetings back and forth. Furthermore, the concluding benediction seems to imply an address to the whole community. The "your" is plural, but "spirit" is singular. In offering such an unusual benediction (see Phlm 25; Gal 6:18), Paul seems to be addressing the congregation as if it were a single group.

The Revised Common Lectionary divides Philippians up into small lections to be read at different times and seasons. No consecutive reading is recommended, and thus the preacher has to be sensitive to the use of the letter in the pulpit. It makes for a wonderful series of sermons and could be used profitably in a combined preaching-teaching setting. The letter calls the community to unity not on the basis of ethnic or family ties, but on the basis of the one story of the Christ, who humbled himself and became obedient unto death on a cross.

---

12. Peterman, *Gift*, 200.

Closing

In other instances, the church often faces efforts to juxtapose competing narratives to understand its oneness and steadfastness. Like athletes in a contest or soldiers in a battle, the church knows that harmony is indispensable. But the model the church follows is often indecisive. Philippians, however, reinforces a unity based on the story of the kenotic Christ, whose reign is supreme and before whom all powers and principalities bow.

PHILEMON

PHILEMON

This brief letter of Paul to a Christian friend, in whose house the church meets, contains only twenty-five verses, but is intriguing beyond measure in the story that it relates and in the appeal it makes concerning Onesimus, a slave being returned to his owner. The fashion in which the letter refers to characters in the story indicates that it is a real letter, and yet it is tantalizing to a modern reader to whom much of the story is allusive. The fact that it deals with the issue of slavery makes it that much more intriguing. The modern reader, as did the nineteenth-century abolitionist, wants Paul to be more aggressive regarding the slave problem, to take the bull by the horns and condemn slavery as an institution. But is that a feasible option for the apostle in the middle part of the first century?

Introduction to Philemon

What is the story behind the letter to Philemon?[1] Paul is in prison (vv. 1, 9, 13), but where we are not specifically told. He, together with his co-sender, Timothy, writes to Philemon, his friend and co-worker, and to Apphia, Archippus, and "to the church in your (singular) house" (v. 2). If Paul were imprisoned in Ephesus,

---

1. Norman R. Petersen, *Rediscovering Paul: Philemon and the Sociology of Paul's Narrative World* (Philadelphia: Fortress Press, 1985), 65–78, in stressing the literary priority of the letter, relates how the story can be told either in a referential sequence or a poetic sequence. The chronological or referential sequence refers to the order in which the events apparently happen. (1) Philemon incurs a debt to Paul (v. 19b); (2) Paul is imprisoned (v. 9; cf. vv. 1, 10, 13, 23); (3) Onesimus runs away and incurs a debt to Philemon (v. 15; cf. 11–13, 18–19a); (4) Onesimus is converted by an imprisoned Paul (v. 10; cf. v. 13); (5) Paul hears of Philemon's love and faith (vv. 4–7); (6) Paul sends Onesimus back to Philemon (v. 12); (7) Paul sends this letter of appeal to Philemon and offers to repay Onesimus's debt (vv. 17–19a); (8) Onesimus and the letter arrive (implied); (9) Philemon responds to Paul's appeal (vv. 20–21); (10) Paul plans to visit Philemon (v. 22). In the literary or poetic sequence, however, the order of events is different. Particularly, for Petersen, the relocation of the acknowledgment of a debt that Onesimus may have incurred to Philemon (vv. 18–19b) and Philemon's incurring of a debt to Paul ("I say nothing about your owing me your very self," v. 19b) become critical in the story of the letter. Though both occur early in the chronological order, their relatively late appearance in the literary sequence, after positive words have been said about both Philemon and Onesimus, makes them the trump card in the letter's argument. The difficulty with Petersen's contention is the heavy load that is placed on indebtedness. Suppose Onesimus had not

as is most likely, then the letter would be dated in the mid-50s. (See Introduction to Philippians.) If he were imprisoned in Rome, then the letter would be dated in the early to mid-60s. Paul actually writes to only one person (see the singular "you" after v. 3), and there is no doubt that that person is Philemon.

Following his usual prayer of thanksgiving for all God has done for Philemon (vv. 4–7), Paul turns to the issue at hand. He makes his appeal in behalf of Onesimus, apparently a slave, who has come under Paul's influence during his imprisonment, and asks that Philemon receive him back "no longer as a slave, but more than a slave, a beloved brother" (v. 16). Paul offers to repay any debts that Onesimus may have incurred with Philemon and reminds Philemon that he is indebted to the apostle, who apparently was instrumental in his conversion to the faith.

Now the story is not as simple as all that. In fact, several details of the story leave the modern reader confused as to the most appropriate reading. For instance, John Knox has argued that because mention of the house church immediately follows the reference to Archippus and since Paul describes Archippus as "our fellow soldier" ("and to Archippus our fellow soldier and to the church in your house," v. 2b), the letter was written to Archippus and not Philemon.[2] Knox proposes that the slave Onesimus was actually owned by Archippus, who lived at Colossae, and the church that gathered in his house was the Colossian church. Paul sent Onesimus home by way of Laodicea, where Philemon lived, with the instructions to read the letter of Colossians as well as the letter to Laodicea (Col 4:15–16). Specifically Paul writes, "And say to Archippus, 'See that you complete the task (*diakonia*) you have received from the Lord'" (Col 4:17). According to Knox the "task" Archippus is to perform is the manumission of Onesimus, in order that he may rejoin Paul as an evangelist. Much of Knox's argument rests on the fact that Ignatius mentions a bishop at Ephesus in the second century by the name of Onesimus, who might have been the same person as the slave, and led to Goodspeed's thesis that Onesimus actually collected the letters of Paul and wrote Ephesians as an introduction.

But Knox's proposal leaves a number of questions unanswered. Is Colossians written by the Apostle Paul? Is it written from Rome, and if so, is it at all

---

absconded with any of his master's funds, but had only sought out Paul as an arbitrator in connection with disputes he may have had with his master (as suggested by Peter Lampe, "Keine 'Sklavenflucht' des Onesimus," *ZNW* 76 [1985]: 135–37); then his indebtedness would only have to do with minor time off from work and not a major amount of money. Petersen is, however, correct in pushing for a consideration of the literary priority of a text over its historical or sociological issues. For another argument for literary priority over historical issues, see Robert Polzin, "Literary and Historical Criticism of the Bible: A Crisis in Scholarship," in *Orientation by Disorientation: Studies in Literary Criticism and Biblical Literary Criticism, Presented in Honor of William A. Beardslee* (ed. Richard A. Spencer; PTMS 35; Pittsburgh, Pa.: Pickwick, 1980), 99–114.

2. John Knox, *Philemon among the Letters of Paul: A New View of Its Place and Importance* (Rev. ed.; New York: Abingdon, 1959), 62–70.

Introduction to Philemon

likely to imagine that Paul, while kept in prison in Rome, could expect in the near future to be a guest in Philemon's home in Asia Minor (Phlm 22)? Is the letter primarily intended for Archippus? The fact that Philemon is mentioned first among the three to whom the letter is addressed would tend to indicate that Philemon is the primary recipient of the letter.

This further raises the issue as to the relationship between Philemon and Onesimus, who is called his "beloved brother," both "in the flesh and in the Lord" (v. 16). Allen Callahan revives a theory developed by abolitionists during antebellum days that "Philemon and Onesimus are indeed brothers both literally and spiritually. They are siblings at odds with each other."[3] This would have enabled the abolitionists to contend that since they were blood brothers Onesimus could not have been a slave of Philemon. It was unusual for relatives to be enslaved.

But there is really no indication that Philemon and Onesimus are blood brothers. Throughout the letter Paul employs family relationships. He speaks of Onesimus being his child, "whose father I have become during my imprisonment" (v. 10). Surely this is a relationship established through the gospel. Over 130 times in the Pauline letters the term *adelphos* is used to designate "fellow Christians"; only twice does Paul speak of "brothers" in a nonmetaphorical sense (Gal 1:19; 1 Cor 9:5). Paul, Philemon, and Onesimus are brothers because Christ is their common Lord. Philemon is asked to receive Onesimus no longer as "a slave but as a beloved brother," and if he refuses to do so, then Philemon is the one not acting like a brother. Petersen contends that "the community, if it is to be consistent with its social structure and its social system, will have no choice but to expel Philemon in order to preserve the brotherhood."[4]

What has caused Onesimus to be separated from Philemon in the first place? Paul offers to repay any indebtedness created by Onesimus (v. 18), which has led a number of scholars to assume that Onesimus was a runaway slave who had absconded with money that rightfully was Philemon's. This would have made Onesimus a fugitive from justice. Apparently a number of slaves in ancient times were clever enough to make off with money from their masters and hide out in large cities where they could blend in with the larger community. In this scenario, the debt Paul offers to pay for Onesimus would involve the money he had taken from his owner.

Sara Winter suggests that Onesimus did not disappear from the house at his own initiative, but rather was sent to be with Paul.[5] Rather than running away, Onesimus was "on loan" to help the apostle during his imprisonment. Paul

---

3. Allen Dwight Callahan, *Embassy of Onesimus: The Letter of Paul to Philemon* (Valley Forge, Pa.: Trinity, 1997), 50–54.
4. Petersen, *Rediscovering Paul*, 99.
5. S. C. Winter, "Paul's Letter to Philemon," *NTS* 33 (1987): 1–12.

wants Onesimus to be released from his obligation to the household in Colossae in order to serve the church in Ephesus. Thus, the letter was written to ask for Onesimus to remain in Ephesus for a longer time. It is hardly possible, however, that a nonbeliever, as Onesimus would have been at the time, would have been sent to serve Paul in the first place. The thesis set forth by Garry Wills proposes that Onesimus was sent to serve Paul in Ephesus, that he came to be a Christian there, and only then confessed that he had defrauded Philemon.[6] This again does not explain why Onesimus as a non-Christian was sent to serve Paul, a missionary for Christ's sake.

Then how does Onesimus meet up with Paul? Though the mention of debt occurs repeatedly in the letter, and, as Petersen contends, in critical locations, it seems difficult to imagine that a fugitive slave like Onesimus, who is a friend of Philemon, would end up in Paul's cell, either in Ephesus or in Rome.[7]

A more plausible explanation comes from Peter Lampe, who has discovered from Roman legal proceedings that when a slave got into difficulty with his or her owner the slave was free to seek out a friend of his or her master, who might intervene for him with his owner.[8] The slave is not trying to escape his owner. Onesimus is not a fugitive from justice, but one who seeks from Paul counsel and advocacy with Philemon. When Onesimus becomes a Christian is not clear, but apparently at the time of Paul's imprisonment since Paul refers to him as "his child" (v. 10) and has sufficient confidence in him to send him back to Philemon (in contradiction to Deut 23:15–16), with the suggestion that he be received as "a beloved brother . . . both in the flesh and in the Lord" (v. 16).

Paul's appeal in behalf of Onesimus is subtle and sensitive. For example, Petersen identifies the roles played by each of the actors in terms of their titles.[9] Onesimus's roles in relation to Paul are child (v. 10) and brother (v. 16). In relation to Philemon, Onesimus is a slave (v. 16), a brother (v. 16), and a debtor (v. 18). The issue is, "Can Philemon continue a master-and-slave relationship with Onesimus, when he is also his brother and the brother and child of Paul?"

---

6. Garry Wills, *What Paul Meant* (New York: Viking, 2006), 112–13.
7. Norman R. Petersen, "Philemon," in *The HarperCollins Bible Commentary* (ed. James Luther Mays and Beverly Roberts Gaventa; rev. ed.; San Francisco: HarperSanFrancisco, 2000), 291–302.
8. Lampe, "Sklavenflucht," 135–37.
9. Petersen, "Philemon," 92.

COMMENTARY

1–3 Salutations

1 Paul, a prisoner[a] of Christ Jesus, and Timothy our brother, to Philemon, our beloved friend and our fellow worker, **2** and to Apphia our[b] sister, to Archippus our fellow soldier, and to the church that meets in your[c] house: **3** Grace to you and peace from God our Father and the Lord Jesus Christ.

    a. One major codex (Bezae) reads "apostle" instead of "prisoner," but this is surely an accommodation to other Pauline epistles (cf. Rom 1:1; 1 Cor 1:1; 2 Cor 1:1; Gal. 1:1).
    b. The Greek reads "the sister," though Apphia may well have been Archippus's sister. Several manuscripts designate her as "beloved sister."
    c. "You" from v. 2 through v. 21 is a singular "you," with the exception of the "grace" in v. 3.

[1] The address follows a typical beginning to a Pauline letter. Paul is, however, in prison, likely where he was when writing the Philippian letter. Since Timothy was also a co-sender of Philippians (cf. Phil 1:1), this would support the notion that Paul's imprisonment was in Ephesus. All the names mentioned in the letter to Philemon (with the exception of Philemon and Apphia) are associated with Colossae, which lies in the Lycus Valley, headed by the major city of Ephesus.

[2–3] Even though the letter is written to Philemon, it is also addressed to the "church in your house" and therefore is a public letter intended for the whole company of believers at Colossae. Paul thus draws on the entire community for support in his concern regarding Onesimus and Philemon. Paul concludes this opening to his letter by expressing the "grace" to the whole community. "Grace and peace from God our Father and the Lord Jesus Christ."

4–7 Thanksgiving

4 I always give thanks to God as I remember you in my prayers, **5** because I heard of your love for all God's people and your faith toward the Lord Jesus. **6** I pray that the partnership of your faith may be effective in the knowledge of every good thing we[a] may do for Christ. **7** I have received much joy and encouragement from your love because the hearts of the saints have been refreshed through you, brother.

    a. The Textus Receptus reads "you" instead of "we"; however, "we" is more expressive, and scribes would have been more likely to change to "you" due to other pronouns in the second person, both singular and plural.[10]

---

10. Bruce M. Metzger, *A Textual Commentary on the Greek New Testament* (London: United Bible Societies, 1994), 588.

[4–5] Paul's prayer of thanksgiving is typical of Pauline letters. In developing the prayer, two things occur. First, Paul establishes rapport with his readers. He recalls the gifts of God to the people in the church: both their love for all people and their "faith toward the Lord Jesus" (v. 5). This has entailed their joining with Paul in the doing of every good deed. Though Paul does not specify what good deeds Philemon has done, Paul is obviously not merely polishing the apple in mentioning Philemon's deeds of love. They have given him great joy and encouragement and have refreshed the hearts of the saints.

[6–7] Second, Paul prays that Philemon's partnership (*koinōnia*) in the faith will be deepened when he can perceive all that they can do for Christ's sake. He, interestingly, does not mention the future, but seems concerned that the Christian faith must manifest itself in deeds of love and that these be for the glory of Christ. His purpose is to stress that Christian faith must manifest itself in love.[11] The following words or ideas in the prayer are picked up in the rest of this short letter: "love" (vv. 5, 9), "fellowship" (vv. 6. 17), "good" (vv. 6, 14), "heart" (vv. 7, 12, 20), "refresh" (vv. 7, 20), "brother" (vv. 7, 20).

8–16 Paul's Prayerful Appeal

8 For this reason, though I am bold enough in Christ to command you to do your duty, 9 yet I prefer to appeal to you on the basis of love. I am nothing other than Paul—an old man[a] and now a prisoner of Christ Jesus. 10 I appeal to you on behalf of my son, whom I have begotten in my bonds, Onesimus. 11 Formerly, he was useless[b] to you, but now he has become useful[b] both to you and to me. 12 I am sending him back,[c] that is my own heart, to you. 13 I wanted[d] to keep him with me so that he might be of service to me in your place during my imprisonment for the gospel. 14 But I preferred to do nothing without your consent, in order that your good deed might be voluntary and not something forced. 15 Perhaps this is the reason he was separated from you for a while, so that you might have him back forever, 16 no longer as a slave but more than a slave, a beloved brother—especially to me but how much more to you, both in the flesh and in the Lord.

a. On occasion translators understand *presbeutēs* ("ambassador") instead of *presbutēs* ("old man"), but Paul is not alluding to any authoritative role. He is forfeiting any opportunity to speak as an apostle.

b. Here Paul is playing on words. Onesimus might have been a "useless" slave to his master, but now he is "useful" to both Paul and to Philemon. He was *achreston*, but now he is *euchreston*.

11. Eduard Lohse, *Colossians and Philemon: A Commentary on the Epistles to the Colossians and to Philemon* (Hermeneia; trans. William R. Poehlmann and Robert J. Karris; Philadelphia: Fortress, 1971), 194–95.

c. Though this verb is in the aorist tense, it is translated as a present. It is an epistolary aorist, as if the writer is taking the stance of the action as it is happening. It is characteristic of letters (e.g., vv. 19, 21; 1 John 2:14).

d. The verb could be rendered as a conative imperfect ("I was trying to keep him with me"), though a narrative imperfect ("Though I was intending to keep him with me") suits just as well.[12]

Paul moves clearly here to make his appeal to Philemon. He states several reasons in the prayer of thanksgiving on which he bases his appeal: Philemon's love for all the saints (v. 5); his faith in Jesus Christ (v. 5); his sharing of the faith (v. 6); the joy and encouragement, which has refreshed the lives of the saints (v. 6).

[8–10] Paul rejects an appeal based on his status as an apostle. "Though I am bold enough to command you to do your duty, yet I would prefer—as an old man and as a prisoner of Jesus Christ," and here we expect Paul to say that Onesimus should be released from his slavery; instead he speaks of Onesimus's conversion. "I am appealing to you for my child, whose father I have become during my imprisonment." What Paul wants is that Philemon receive Onesimus as a brother. He presses the brotherly connection while never asking for Onesimus's release.

[11–14] "Formerly" he was useless to you, but now as my son he would render enormous service to me "in your place" during my imprisonment for the gospel. Exactly what is meant by the play on words ("Onesimus" means "useful") is difficult to tell. In what sense was Onesimus useless to Philemon? "Useless" was a common term for bad slaves, and maybe Onesimus had been a bad slave. Those who take the scenario that he had absconded with some of Philemon's money find a reference to that here; however, that seems a bit farfetched. It is certainly clear that Paul has found him useful in the work of the gospel and has found him particularly helpful in ways Philemon could not be.

Paul is faced with several options as to what to do with Onesimus. One is that he could keep Onesimus with him as a fellow worker in the gospel, and simply finesse his relationship with Philemon. Apparently he would have had no trouble from the Roman authorities or with Philemon. This would seem to be the natural and logical action to take.

[15–16] And yet to do so would prevent Philemon from experiencing the reconciliation that could take place between a Christian slave and a brother, something Paul had himself experienced. "Perhaps this is why he was separated from you, so that you could have him back no longer as a slave but much more than a slave, a beloved brother" (vv. 15–16).

We are not told how Onesimus came to Christ, but Paul was clearly involved. He treated Onesimus as a son after his conversion and calls him "my heart"

---

12. See Winter, "Philemon," 7–9.

(v. 12), and though we are not told anything about Onesimus's feelings toward Philemon, one could anticipate his desire to be reconciled to his former owner. Paul seems eager to facilitate this reconciliation, even at the expense of no longer having Onesimus as an aide in his ministry.

17–21 Paul's Confidence in Philemon's Response

17 So if you count me your partner, welcome him as you would welcome me.

18 And if he has done anything wrong or owes you money, charge it to my account. 19 I, Paul, am writing[a] this with my own hand, I will repay it. Not to mention that you owe me your very self. 20 Yes, brother. Let me have this benefit from you in the Lord. Refresh my heart in Christ.

21 Confident of your obedience, I am writing[a] to you, knowing that you will do even more than I say.

a. Other examples of the epistolary aorist (see v. 12), which are translated in the present tense.

Paul anticipates that the situation will work out to Onesimus's advantage. His friendship with Philemon (v. 17), his patron-client relationship with him (vv. 19–21), as well as the fact that Onesimus has become a brother in the faith (v. 16), and Paul's very dear "son" (v. 10)—all make Paul confident that Philemon will act positively toward Onesimus and that he will "do even more than I say" (v. 21). What that "more" might entail is anybody's guess. It might mean that Onesimus is allowed to serve with Paul in his prison ministry, that he become a fellow worker (vv. 19–21) or that he be freed from slavery. But at heart Paul is concerned that Philemon receive him as a brother and so be reconciled to Onesimus. If manumission is intended, it is certainly very subtly implied. Paul may leave the suggestion so vague because he himself does not know what is the best course of action and thus leaves it open to Philemon to discern.[13]

The context between the ethical dilemma that faced Paul and the modern situation of slavery is very different. It is estimated that about a quarter to a third of urban populations in the first century were made up of slaves. As they had the opportunity, Paul encouraged slaves to seek their freedom (1 Cor 7:20–21), but he does not instigate a revolt, nor does he push for Onesimus's immediate release.

22–25 Paul's Travel Plans and Greetings from Friends

22 One thing more—prepare for me a guest room, for I am hoping through your prayers to be restored to you. 23 Epaphras, my fellow prisoner in

---

13. John M. G. Barclay, "Paul, Philemon and the Dilemma of Christian Slave-Ownership," *NTS* 37 (1991): 174–75.

Paul's Travel Plans and Greetings from Friends 105

Christ Jesus, sends you greetings. 24 And so do Mark, Aristarchus, Demas, and Luke, my fellow workers. 25 The grace of the Lord Jesus Christ be with your spirit.

[22] The letter draws to a close, as do most of Paul's letters, with his travel plans and with greetings from a number of fellow workers and with a "grace," except that here his intentions to come to visit Philemon function to confirm the pressing decision he has to make. Will he act as an angry slave owner, or will he treat Onesimus as a "beloved brother"? His plan to pay a visit is clearly made with the intention of discovering what has ensued regarding Onesimus. Paul, of course, cannot tell how soon that will be since he remains in prison and cannot make a specific promise as to when he will come to visit. But his intentions are clear that he wishes to return to Colossae and to learn what has happened to Onesimus and Philemon. Did this hoped-for reconciliation take place?

[23–25] Furthermore, the sending of greetings from this group who were apparently in prison with Paul (all of whom are mentioned in Colossians) is a reminder that others (as are those who are also saints in the church that meets in Philemon's house) are also observing Philemon's actions. Philemon's response will not be a solo act, but will be done in the context of the church.

Paul and Slave Ownership

Should Paul have taken a lead in pressuring Philemon into manumitting Onesimus? This sounds like an obvious and attractive option, until one imagines the reaction of other slaves Philemon owns. Would they not be outraged as they had to remain in slavery when this one who had been converted was freed? Furthermore, any other slaves who were Christians and accepted their freedom would then leave the church without a proper location for its meetings. Paul depended on houses of sufficient size to provide the church with adequate meeting space for its gatherings, and those homes depended on Christian slave owners. Slavery was built into the very fabric of Greco-Roman society.

Paul did not lead a revolt against the slave system in his dealings with Philemon and Onesimus. In fact, he makes no plea for the manumission of Onesimus. Not a single word expresses the wish or the command that Onesimus be legally emancipated, nor is Philemon condemned for the fact that he owned a slave.

One has to ask, "What then does Paul have in mind for Onesimus if manumission is not his target?" Verse 13 says that Paul wants Onesimus "to serve with me during my imprisonment for the gospel." Paul's expectation that Philemon will treat Onesimus "as a beloved brother" (v. 16) and that he would welcome Onesimus as he would himself (v. 17) lays out an entirely new structure of relationships between the two, relationships that can be seen in marked contrast to that of the typical slave and owner. The Christian gospel in which there is neither Jew nor Greek, bond nor free, male and female, but all are one in Christ Jesus (Gal 3: 28) becomes determinative for their relationship.

While Paul does not advocate the manumission of Onesimus, he nevertheless preaches more than an apolitical gospel. He proclaims a kingdom of a different sort, the kingdom of God and of his Christ. "The death of Christ brings about the transfer of believers from enslavement to sin to the service of Christ as their Lord and Master (1 Cor 6:19–20; 7:21–23; cf. Rom 3:24; 8:15–21; Gal 3:13, where 'redemption' is a purchase from enslavement)."[14] Therefore, acting as a brother to brothers in the faith becomes essential to life in the kingdom of God, and failure to demonstrate brotherly affection puts in jeopardy one's status both in the church and in the kingdom of God.

---

14. Petersen, "Philemon," 1147.

INDEX OF ANCIENT SOURCES

OLD TESTAMENT

Genesis
1:26–27	53
1:27	54
1:28	58
3:5	53
9:2	61

Exodus
15:16	61
16:1–12	61n49
17:1–7	61n49
29:38–41	63
32:32	82

Leviticus
12:3	71
16:29	49

Numbers
6:24–26	86
12:7	24
28:1–8	63

Deuteronomy
2:25	61
3:25	62
10:16	69
23:15–16	98
30:6	69
32:5 (LXX)	62

1 Samuel
7:43	16

2 Kings
14:25	24

Nehemiah
10:29	24

Job
13:16	37

Psalms
8:6	81
19:1	31
34:18	85
37:8–9	49
38:9–10	49
45:20–25	81
69:28	82
88:21 (LXX)	24
89:20	24
110:1	81
145:18	85

Isaiah
6:3	31
42:6	62
45	58
45:21–23	58
45:23	51, 58
49:1	73
49:6	62, 73
52:13	53
52:13–53:12	53
58:3	49
58:5	49

Jeremiah
1:5	73
4:4	69
9:22–23	69
9:25–26	69
25:4	24

Daniel
12:1	82

Amos
3:7	24
5:18–20	30

Habakkuk
3:3	31

NEW TESTAMENT

Matthew
5:14–15	62
9:37–38	16
10:10	16
11:29	49
22:44	81
26:64	81

Mark
12:36	81
14:62	81

Luke
20:42–43	81
22:69	81

Acts
2:34–35	81
5:34	71
13:5	6
13:14–15	6
13:43	5n3
13:47	62
13:50	5n3
16	10
16:1–3	65
16:6–10	6
16:7	59
16:11–12	4–5
16:11–39	5
16:11–40	23
16:12	4
16:14	5
16:17	5
16:19–24	15, 47
16:22–24	6
16:40	5
17:1–2	6
17:4	5n3
17:10	6
17:14–15	23
17:17	5n3
18:4	6
18:7	5n3
19:8	6
20:3–6	65
22:3	71
23:23–26:32	10
24:16	31
28:16–31	9

Romans
1:1	24, 101
1:7	24

Index of Ancient Sources

Romans (*continued*)
1:8	27
1:13	12, 33
1:21	61
2:25–29	69
3:23	31
3:24	106
5:1–2	26
5:1–5	84
5:2	31
5:11	69
6:1–11	77
8:6	70
8:15	57
8:18–39	46
8:19–20	38
8:23–24	38
8:31–39	52
8:34	81
12:1	48, 85
12:2	31
12:6–8	26
12:9	31
13:13	44
15	10
15:12–21	53
15:13	85
15:22–29	9
15:22–33	64
16:1	25

1 Corinthians
1:1	24, 101
1:2	24
1:1–17	18
1:10–2:5	79
1:18	57
1:18–2:16	18
1:30	25
1:31	69
2:3	61
3:5	25
4:9–13	46
5:6–8	41
6:19–20	106
7:20–21	104
7:21–23	106
7:39	40
8:6	58
9:5	97
10:10	61
10:32	31
11:1	78
11:30	40
12:8–10	26
12:28–30	26
13	52
15:1–11	30n16
15:6	40
15:15	40

15:20	40
15:20–28	77
15:21–22	53
15:25	81
15:35–55	39
15:44–49	53
15:50	69
15:51	40, 81
16:5–9	64
16:22	85

2 Corinthians
1:1	24–25, 101
1:3	48
1:8	33
1:8–9	10
1:8–10	10
1:9	6
2:8	12
4:7–12	46
4:10	46
5:16	69
6:5	10
7:15	61
8:1–5	3
8:2	89
8:9	55
10:17	69
11:7–9	89
11:12–13	15n26
11:14	15n26
11:18	69
11:22	72
11:23	10, 25
11:23–29	46
12:12	15n26
13:1–2	15n26
13:10	64

Galatians
1:1	24, 101
1:6–7	30n16
1:6–9	36n10
1:11	12
1:13–14	71
1:15–16	72
3:1–3	36n10
3:13	106
4:8–9	57
4:19–21	36n10
5:1–4	36n10
5:6	69
5:12	36n10, 68
5:16	44
5:19–21	70
6:12	46, 79
6:15	69
6:18	90

Ephesians
1:20	81

2:8–10	61
4:11	26
6:5	61

Philippians
1:1	28, 51, 65, 101
1:1–2	23–26
1:1–3:1	7, 8n7
1:1–3:1a	67
1:2	58
1:3	28
1:3–5	62
1:3–7	48
1:3–8	23, 26, 28–30
1:3–11	8, 8n11, 26–31, 82, 88
1:4	19, 28, 84
1:5	7, 12, 18, 28, 29, 30, 35, 47
1:6	18, 28, 29, 30, 31, 40, 61
1:7	9, 12, 28–29, 35, 38, 88
1:7–8	12
1:7–2:4	12
1:8	28–29, 48
1:9	28
1:9–10	77
1:9–11	23, 27, 30–31
1:10	18, 28, 30, 40
1:11	31
1:12	28, 32, 33, 35, 43
1:12–14	28, 32–35
1:12–26	11, 13, 17, 32–41, 42, 45
1:13	9, 33, 34, 45, 90
1:14	9, 34, 58
1:15–17a	35
1:15–18a	35–37
1:15–18	15, 17, 29, 49
1:16	28, 38
1:17	9, 49
1:18	28, 32, 36–37, 68, 84
1:18b	38
1:18b–26	37–41
1:19	37–38
1:19–24	10, 39
1:19–26	12, 28
1:20–26	10
1:21	39
1:21–22	19
1:21–23	41
1:21–24	38–41
1:22	39, 40
1:23	38, 39, 41
1:24	41, 69–70
1:25	28, 32, 33, 35, 38, 39, 41, 84
1:25–26	10, 39, 41
1:26	41, 51

Index of Ancient Sources

1:27	13, 13n23, 15, 28, 34, 43, 44, 59, 64, 82	2:19–23	13, 64	3:18–19	78–79
		2:19–24	23, 64–65	3:18–20	14
		2:19–30	64–67	3:19	16–17, 28
1:27–28	44–46	2:19–3:1	70	3:20	18, 43, 44, 58, 85
1:27–29	75	2:20	65, 66	3:20–21	18, 28, 40, 41, 79–81
1:27–30	12, 15, 17, 29, 30, 42–47, 48, 49, 81	2:20–21	19, 65		
		2:21–22	14	3:21	49, 81, 85
		2:22	28, 65	4:1	3, 12, 19, 28, 49, 58, 67, 83, 84, 85
1:27–2:18	11, 13, 31, 42–63	2:24	9, 64, 66–67, 70		
		2:25–29	64	4:1–3	82–83
1:28	19	2:25–30	7, 11, 13, 17, 65–67	4:2	12, 19, 28, 58, 62, 83, 85
1:28b	44				
1:28–30	18	2:26	28, 66	4:2–3	17–18, 25–26, 45, 82
1:29	46, 75	2:27–28	66		
1:29–30	6	2:28	28	4:2–7	67
1:30	12, 28, 40, 43, 45, 46–47	2:28–29	20, 84	4:3	5, 28, 83
		2:29	28, 58, 66, 70	4:3–4	29
2:1	12, 28, 29, 43	2:30	19, 66, 67, 68, 79	4:4	28, 29, 58, 67, 68, 84, 85
2:1–2	19, 28, 47	3:1	7–8, 28, 67–68, 70, 84		
2:1–4	47–49, 55, 65			4:4–6	13, 64
2:1–5	54, 55	3:1–2	7–8, 67–69	4:4–7	8n7
2:1–11	47–59	3:1–4a	67–70	4:4–9	7, 84–87
2:1–18	59	3:1–4:3	67–83	4:4–23	84–91
2:2	12, 28, 47, 51, 83, 84	3:1a	67	4:5	18, 58, 85, 87
		3:1b	8, 67, 68	4:5–6	85–86
2:2–4	13, 64	3:1b–4:1	67	4:6	85
2:3	49	3:2	7–8, 12, 14, 16–17, 68	4:7	51, 86
2:3–4	19, 47–49			4:8	28, 67, 86
2:4	65	3:2–3	70	4:8–9	8n7, 13, 64, 67, 86–87
2:5	12, 18, 28, 49, 51–52, 55–56, 59, 79	3:2–4	14		
		3:2–21	7n6	4:9	86–87
2:5–11	50–59	3:2–4:3	7–8, 8n7	4:10	19, 28, 58, 68, 84, 88–89
2:6–11	13, 18, 50, 52–59, 66, 73, 80, 81	3:3	51, 70		
		3:3–4a	69–70	4:10–20	7–8, 8n7, 11–12, 17, 29, 67, 87–90
2:6	52, 54–55	3:4–11	72		
2:6–8	52–58	3:4b–5d	71		
2:7	45, 53, 57, 65	3:4b–6	71–72	4:11–12	89
2:8	49, 50, 52, 66, 74, 79	3:4b–16	70–77	4:11–13	87, 89
2:9	46	3:5e–6	71	4:11–14	19
2:9–11	19, 53, 54, 55, 58–59, 79	3:7	72	4:12	19
		3:7–8	72–73, 76	4:13	19
2:10	51, 52	3:7–11	73	4:14	12, 28
2:10–11	58	3:8	58, 72–73	4:15	12, 28
2:11	52, 58	3:9	39, 73–74	4:15–19	89–90
2:12	12, 28, 60, 61	3:10	12, 19, 28, 29, 33, 39, 40, 46, 74–75, 79	4:16	6
2:12–13	59–61			4:17	89
2:12–15	13, 64	3:10–11	74–75	4:18	7, 89
2:12–18	59–63	3:11	40, 77	4:19	49, 51, 89–90
2:13	61	3:11–12	28	4:20–23	7
2:14	60, 62	3:12	76, 77	4:21	28
2:14–15	61–63	3:12–14	76, 77	4:21–23	8n7, 67, 90–91
2:14–18	59	3:12–16	75–77	4:22	9, 10, 45
2:15	30, 62	3:13	76	4:23	58
2:16	18, 28, 40, 62–63	3:14	40, 51, 75, 76–77, 79		
2:16a	62	3:15	28, 75, 79	**Colossians**	
2:17	28, 63	3:15–16	77	1:15–20	55
2:17–18	12, 20, 28, 29, 63, 68, 84, 85	3:16	77	3:1	81
		3:17	14, 17, 40, 44, 75	4:12	24
2:18	63	3:17–19	12, 77–79	4:15–16	96
2:19	58, 70	3:18	14, 16, 68	4:16	96

1 Thessalonians

1:6–10	30
1:7	27
2:1	12–13, 33
2:2	6
2:2–4	47
2:12	44
2:19–20	63
4:12	44
4:13–15	40
4:13–5:10	39
4:15	39

1 Timothy

3:1–2	25

2 Timothy

2:24	24

Titus

1:1	24

Philemon

1	95, 95n1, 101
1–3	101
2	95, 101
2–3	101
2b	96
3	101
4–5	102
4–7	95n1, 96, 101–2
5	102–3
6	102–3
6–7	102
7	27, 102
8–10	103
8–16	102–4
9	95, 95n1, 102
10	95n1, 96, 98, 104
11–13	95n1
11–14	103
12	95n1, 102, 103–4
13	95, 95n1, 105
14	102
15	95n1, 97
15–16	103–4
16	96–98, 103, 104, 105
17	102, 104, 105
17–19a	95n1
17–21	104
18	97–98
18–19a	95n1
18–19b	95n1
19	103
19–21	104
19b	95n1
20	102
20–21	95n1
21	101, 103, 104
22	64, 97, 95n1, 105
22–25	104–5
23	95n1
23–24	101
23–25	105
25	90

Hebrews

1:3	81
1:13	81
8:1	81
10:12	81

James

1:1	24

1 Peter

1:17	31

2 Peter

1:1	24

1 John

2:14	103

Jude

1	24

Revelation

20:12–15	82

APOCRYPHA

Wisdom of Solomon

2:23–24	53

1 Maccabees

1:51	25

DEAD SEA SCROLLS

Hodayot (Thanksgiving Hymns)

1QH 5:13–22	49

Serek Hayaḥad (Rule of the Community)

1QS 5:3–4	49

GRECO-ROMAN LITERATURE

ARISTOTLE

Nicomachean Ethics

8.13.9	89

Rhetoric

2.20	63
1393a	63
1394a	63

CICERO

Rhetorica ad Herenniun

4.30	39n19

DIO CHRYSOSTOM

De dei Cognitione

17.2	68

Orations (Discourses)

3.14–15	68
3.25–26	68
55.4, 5	78n26

HOMER

Iliad

9.489	60
22.83	60

Odyssey

8	25
163	25

ISOCRATES

Nicocles

12	68
40	68

PSEUDO-LABANIUS

Epistolary Styles

52	13, 64

SENECA

Ad Lucilium

9.23	89

TACITUS

Annales

1:3–4	34n6
2:15	34n2

EARLY CHRISTIAN LITERATURE

IGNATIUS

To the Romans

4:1–3	40

INDEX OF AUTHORS AND SUBJECTS

Alexander, Loveday, 13, 42–43

Barth, Karl, 26n8, 40, 45, 50, 61, 74–75, 82, 84, 86
Bassler, Jouette M., 70
Bauckham, Richard, 58
Baur, Ferdinand Christian, 7
Bockmuehl, Markus N., 11n18, 15, 38, 53n22, 77
Brewer, R. R., 44
Bultmann, Rudolf, 56, 69–70, 85n3

Caird, G. B., 40, 53n22, 54n27, 70, 76–77, 81n35, 89
Callahan, Allen Dwight, 97
Calvin, John, 84–85
Christ hymn, 18–19, 45, 50–59, 65, 73, 80
Christology, 51–52, 54, 58
circumcision, 16, 67–71
Collange, Jean-François, 11n18, 23, 67, 82
compassion, 27–29, 47–48
Croy, N. Clayton, 39

deacons, 23–26
D'Angelo, Mary Rose, 83
De Vos, Craig Steven, 4n2, 44–45
Dunn, James D. G., 54, 58

"Enemies of the Cross," 3, 14, 16–17, 77–81
Epaphroditus, 3, 5, 7–9, 11, 13, 17, 19–20, 29, 64–68, 70, 78–79, 82–83, 87–89
eschatology, 17–18, 28, 30, 38–41, 57–58, 60, 63, 73, 77, 80, 85
Euodia and Syntyche, 6, 25–26, 82–85

Fee, Gordon D., 10n16, 11n18, 12n21, 43n1, 53n22, 82
Fowl, Stephen, 56, 63, 69, 81n36

Garland, David E., 8

Hawthorne, Gerald F., 10n17, 11n18, 30n16, 44, 66
Hays, Richard B., 38n14, 73
Hooker, Morna D., 9, 11n18, 16n32, 27, 33n1, 52n20, 78n27, 80n31

Hurtado, Larry W., 16n31, 56

imprisonment, 9–11, 15, 19, 28, 32–33, 38–42, 95–98, 101–5

Jewett, Robert, 15
joy, 3, 8, 19–20, 28–29, 37–39, 41, 48–49, 63, 67, 84–85, 88

Käsemann, Ernst, 51n12, 56–58
Kilpatrick, G. D., 16, 68
Kittredge, Cynthia Briggs, 83
Knox, John, 96
Kuhn, T. S., 56

Lampe, Peter, 96n1, 98
Lightfoot, J. B., 10n16, 25n5, 28, 58–59, 82, 83
Lincoln, Andrew T., 41, 80
Lohmeyer, Ernst, 10n17, 11n18, 40, 52n17, 55, 75n19, 80n29, 87
love, 26–28, 30–32, 47–49, 101–3

Malherbe, Abraham J., 11n19, 68
Marshall, Peter, 12n21, 83, 89
Martin, Dale, 24
Martin, Ralph P., 43n1, 51, 52n19, 53n21, 57n36, 59n45, 86n6
Meeks, Wayne A., 5n2, 19n38, 26, 52
Metzger, Bruce M., 4n1, 51, 69n6, 76, 101n10
mind, 51, 55–56, 79, 83
Mitchell, Margaret, 34

O'Brien, Peter T., 11n18, 24n3, 27n10, 29n15, 34, 36n8,
Oakes, Peter, 4n2, 81
opponents, 14–17, 33–34, 79

participation, 3, 12, 19, 26–29, 46–48, 72, 74–75, 84, 88
peace, 84, 86–87
Peterlin, Davorin, 25–26, 28n14, 82
Peterman, Gerald, 8, 88, 90n12
Petersen, Norman R., 95n1, 97–98, 106n14
Philippi, 3–6, 9–11, 15, 35, 45, 64–65
prayer, 26–28, 102–4

resurrection, 52–53, 74–75, 77–78
Reumann, John, 12, 25n5, 80
Rome, 9–11, 15, 18, 44, 80–81, 90, 96–98

salutation, 12, 23–24, 101
salvation, 29–30, 37–38, 45, 50–52, 59–61
Sanders, E. P., 71
Schubert, Paul, 28
Schütz, John Howard, 36
Schweizer, Eduard, 48
slavery, 95, 103–6
Stanton, Graham, 34–35
Stendahl, Krister, 73
suffering, 6, 8, 18, 24, 33, 37–39, 46–47, 53, 74–75, 77–79

Sumney, Jerry L., 16n33, 79

thanksgiving
  in Philemon, 96, 101–3
  in Philippians, 3, 7–8, 12–13, 26–30, 61, 85–89
Timothy, 4, 8, 13, 19, 23–24, 26, 64–66, 68, 70, 78, 82–83, 95

unity, 8, 11, 19, 42, 45, 47–49, 59–61, 82

Ware, James P., 60n46, 62–63
Wills, Gary, 98
Winter, S. C., 44, 97, 103n12
Wright, N. T., 41n24, 58